CultureShock!
A Survival Guide to Customs and Etiquette

Syria

Coleman South

Marshall Cavendish
Editions

This 4th edition published in 2011 by:
Marshall Cavendish Corporation
99 White Plains Road
Tarrytown, NY 10591-9001
www.marshallcavendish.us

First published in 1995 by Times Editions Pte Ltd, reprinted 1996, 1997, 1998; 2nd edition published in 2001; 3rd edition published in 2008 by Marshall Cavendish International (Asia) Private Limited.

Other Marshall Cavendish Offices:
Marshall Cavendish International (Asia) Private Limited. 1 New Industrial Road, Singapore 536196 ■ Marshall Cavendish International. PO Box 65829, London EC1P 1NY, UK ■ Marshall Cavendish International (Thailand) Co Ltd. 253 Asoke, 12th Flr, Sukhumvit 21 Road, Klongtoey Nua, Wattana, Bangkok 10110, Thailand ■ Marshall Cavendish (Malaysia) Sdn Bhd, Times Subang, Lot 46, Subang Hi-Tech Industrial Park, Batu Tiga, 40000 Shah Alam, Selangor Darul Ehsan, Malaysia

Marshall Cavendish is a trademark of Times Publishing Limited

IISBN 13: 978-0-7614-5880-7

Please contact the publisher for the Library of Congress catalog number

Printed in Singapore by Times Printers Pte Ltd

Photo Credits:
All black and white photos by the author. Colour photos from Photolibrary.
■ Cover photo: Photolibrary

All illustrations by TRIGG

ABOUT THE SERIES

Culture shock is a state of disorientation that can come over anyone who has been thrust into unknown surroundings, away from one's comfort zone. *CultureShock!* is a series of trusted and reputed guides which has, for decades, been helping expatriates and long-term visitors to cushion the impact of culture shock whenever they move to a new country.

Written by people who have lived in the country and experienced culture shock themselves, the authors share all the information necessary for anyone to cope with these feelings of disorientation more effectively. The guides are written in a style that is easy to read and cover a range of topics that will arm readers with enough advice, hints and tips to make their lives as normal as possible again.

Each book is structured in the same manner. It begins with the first impressions that visitors will have of that city or country. To understand a culture, one must first understand the people—where they came from, who they are, the values and traditions they live by, as well as their customs and etiquette. This is covered in the first half of the book.

Then on with the practical aspects—how to settle in with the greatest of ease. Authors walk readers through topics such as how to find accommodation, get the utilities and telecommunications up and running, enrol the children in school and keep in the pink of health. But that's not all. Once the essentials are out of the way, venture out and try the food, enjoy more of the culture and travel to other areas. Then be immersed in the language of the country before discovering more about the business side of things.

To round off, snippets of basic information are offered before readers are 'tested' on customs and etiquette of the country. Useful words and phrases, a comprehensive resource guide and list of books for further research are also included for easy reference.

CONTENTS

PREFACE

In the early 1990s I finished an M.A. in TESOL (Teaching English to Speakers of other Languages) with the specific intent of living and teaching overseas—a mid-life career change. I got my first job teaching English overseas in Damascus and began searching both the local public library and the library at my university for up-to-date information about Syria and found next to nothing. My university had 17,000 students and the metro area of the public library had over a million people, yet what little printed material I could find about Syria was either terribly dated or written by ex-CIA staffers who had served time there; and all of it was political or historical material that told nothing of what to expect as a resident of modern Syria, how to behave, what I should take with me, etc. The purpose of this book is to help others going to Syria for the first time with not only cultural information, but with information about daily living there.

It is assumed that the reader knows little or nothing about Syria, and even those who have lived in the Persian Gulf states, Israel, Turkey, or other countries of the region, are in for some surprises in Syria. There's no other place like it, not even Jordan or Lebanon. While living there, I often got the feeling that I resided in a living museum, yet there's a certain vitality of life that seems as new as it is timeless. Syria does things in its own way and in its own time. This book should help not only those who plan to live in Syria, but also those who plan to travel in the country, containing as it does some intimate information that is not included in the few travel guides one can buy for Syria.

There's one rather substantial caveat, though: I am Caucasian and thus my personal experiences with Syrians reflect that. Why is that important? Because sadly, Arabs in general and Syrians along with the rest of them, can be racist, basing their prejudice primarily on skin colour and secondly on country of origin. Arab culture seems to have a totem pole in which White Westerners are at the top with Arabs being nearly equal or slightly below them; at the absolute bottom are Black Africans, with lighter-skinned Blacks from Western countries being just slightly above the Africans. Those who typically do the lowest-level jobs in rich Arab societies such as servants, nannies, maids, road workers, etc. (Sri Lankans, Filipinos/as, Bangladeshis and Pakistanis) are also near the bottom of this social totem. Similarly, darker-skinned Hispanics and Chinese, Koreans or Japanese (many of whom may be mistaken as Filipinos/as or Southeast Asians) will also likely not be treated as well as I was by many Syrians, but they seem to put the lighter-skinned people from eastern Asian groups up higher on their totem pole. When I was in Damascus, I knew a Black American student who actually got spit at a couple of times and had insults hurled at him from passing cars. He also had trouble finding a place to live as most landlords/rental agents didn't want to rent to him. On the other hand, a Japanese acquaintance who was quite light-skinned seemed to be treated similarly to me. I hate to make broad generalisations such as this one and to accuse a whole group of people of such negative characteristics (and of course, not all Syrians will react negatively to you), but it was not uncommon for those of darker skin to have unpleasant experiences with some Syrian people based on their skin color. This may, however, have changed for the better in recent times.

I want to thank my friend Samer of Damascus for his assistance and information plus the many nameless Syrians from whom I learned so much about their culture, beliefs and way of life. I also want to thank the Marshall Cavendish staff in general and specifically the editors Sylvy Soh and Melvin Neo for their assistance at various stages of this revision.

MAP OF SYRIA

FIRST IMPRESSIONS

CHAPTER 1

'We're not in Kansas anymore, Toto.'
—Dorothy, in *The Wizard of Oz*

I WAS TALKING WITH A YOUNG SYRIAN FRIEND about the peculiarities of Syrian Arab Airlines (or just Syrian Air, as it's usually called), and he laughed and said, "Well, there's only one Syria, so there's only one Syrian Air!" *There's only one Syria* summarises more than you can imagine unless you've lived or travelled in Syria for a while, for the uniqueness of the place will strike you immediately.

COMING IN FOR A LANDING

As you fly into Damascus, one of the first oddities you might notice is that regardless of where the aircraft enters Syrian airspace, it travels far inland, then approaches Damascus from the east. This means that even though Damascus is only a few minutes by air from the Mediterranean, you'll travel over land for about an hour before you touch down.

There are various explanations for this. One is that the Syrians—surrounded by less-than-friendly nations—simply do not allow air traffic anywhere over the capital city. The airport is 32 km (20 miles) from the city and surrounded by military installations. This way, the government will be better protected from potential enemies both internal and external. At any rate, Damascus may be the world's only capital city with no air traffic overhead. In nearly three years there I did not see or hear commercial aircraft more than a few times. Imagine endless blue summer skies with never a jet contrail in sight; it's a strange feeling.

Customs

Be prepared to spend up to 40 minutes or so going through several passport checkpoints. At one of those points, one of the landing cards you fill out is stamped and returned to you along with your passport. Make sure you keep it: if you try to leave the country without it, you'll be hassled and probably end up paying a "fee", which varies depending on the customs agent you encounter at the time. After you've cleared the first window, you pass through a gate where another branch of the government can look at your passport, then on to the baggage claim area. Damascus International Airport is old but has had some renovation. The arrival hall and baggage carousels are still old and worn, however. If you have a lot of luggage, a baggage cart will cost you about 50 Syrian pounds (SP, but also called *lira* for some reason unknown to me), which is roughly US$ 1. After you load it, you head for the customs inspection counter.

If you're lucky, the customs people will just wave you on through—at least that's what I've experienced on most of my trips to Syria. If not, they probably won't search your luggage thoroughly. What they look for primarily are electronics and drugs. If they find electronics, they may want a customs tax. The first time I came through, only one large trunk (out of seven pieces of luggage) was inspected. A boom box stereo was in it and several agents examined it, consulting among themselves for a while before giving it back to me saying, "OK, this time." They asked what was in another large box (a guitar and cassette tapes) and then waved me on. They seem to be particularly accomodating to visitors from Western countries and willing to make their entry as easy as possible.

Leaving the Airport

After you leave the customs area and enter the lobby, you will get your first taste of Syrian variety. People of nearly every colour and mode of dress will be in a human crush awaiting arrivals. The airport is often busy and crowded (an estimated 3.6 million visitors went through it in 2008), and most users are from the Middle East and North Africa, it seems, so you will see great variety of costume and appearance.

Unless someone is there to pick you up, taxi drivers will approach you from every direction saying, "Taxi?" and before you even accept an offer, one of them is likely to grab your cart and start wheeling it out. You should ask for the fare, and not pay more than about 500 SP or the equivalent of US$ 10 for a ride to the city (you can often bargain for 300–400 SP).

If no taxi driver approaches you, or if you don't want to haggle over price, go to one of the rental car windows or to the taxi stand and ask for a taxi to Damascus, but bargain

Watch Your Bags

Before you get to the taxi, one or more of the luggage boys who work for tips may grab your cart, take it to the taxi, and load your things into it—with extreme carelessness if you don't demand otherwise. Don't pay them more than about 25 SP.

with them, because they will want two to three times as much as a regular city taxi—often in hard currency. Karnak, Syria's national bus system, also travels from the aiport to the bus centre in an area called Baramkeh, but that's not a reasonable option if you have lots of luggage.

If no one is meeting you, it might be wise to exchange a little foreign currency at the airport; the rate is the same as at the bank, and it will give you some local cash for food and taxi fare. There's an ATM for cash withdrawals and several exchange bureaus in the exit lobby.

DAMASCUS: STREETS AND SIDEWALKS

The road to Damascus from the airport is usually not crowded and is lined on both sides by trees. But as soon as you reach the edge of the city, the peacefulness will end. Many people told me that Cairo had the noisiest and most disorderly traffic in the world; but I spent a week there and saw or heard nothing worse than what I did every day in central Damascus. The traffic defines chaos and din. Traffic police are stationed at every major intersection that has a traffic light; otherwise, most drivers would ignore the signals, barrelling through a red light with their horn blaring and lights flashing to say, "Look out, I'm coming through!"

Traffic

There are thousands more vehicles than the city has room for, and they come at each other from every conceivable direction, including the wrong way on one-way streets and on the wrong side of two-way streets. Not a street in Damascus is straight for long, and few of them meet at right angles; the busiest intersections are traffic circles much like in Great Britain, except these are not British drivers.

The cars, trucks, buses, pedestrians, antiquated Chinese bicycles, horsedrawn carts, motorcycles, donkeys saddled with bags of vegetables and micro-pickups all weave a choreography that makes the head spin. Vehicles drive within a few centimetres of each other and completely ignore any lanes marked on the roadway; yet amazingly, this jumble creates relatively few serious accidents. On the other hand, you seldom see cars that have travelled these wicked streets for long without nicks, dents and scratches.

Another factor in the general traffic confusion is the raging noise. To begin with, many vehicles have no mufflers. Then, Syrians honk their horns at everything and nothing. (Former Monty Python member Michael Palin, commented that Egyptian horns were hooked to both brake and gas pedals—an appropriate description of Syria, as well.) When

you're walking the streets or sidewalks, the din actually hurts, and I often had to cover my ears. No matter where you cross the street, drivers will beep at you; if a man sees a scarfless woman he considers attractive, he beeps (this is especially true of taxi drivers); if they think another driver is even thinking about pulling in front of them, they toot their horns; and before a traffic light ever has a chance to turn green (the lights here go from red to yellow, then to green) the blare of horns is deafening. To say that this culture loves auto horns is an understatement. I have heard blasting car horns attached to motorcycles and even bicycles. Many of the buses and cars have special high-decibel or musical horns. Some play whole stanzas of popular music, some sound like sirens, and others play bizarre selections of seemingly random notes. I've even heard a Jingle Bells horn and one that played a medley of Christmas music! To live in this racket can be maddening, but it is entertaining at times.

First Stop

Syria has precious few mid-range hotels, so you'll probably either be staying at a flop house or a US$ 250 per night (and up) luxury hotel, although there is now a youth hostel, as well.

The luxury Cham Hotel on the Cote Azur of Syria, north of Latakia.

When choosing a hotel, keep in mind that the lobbies are usually much more luxurious than the rooms. Ask to see your room before agreeing to it. Unless you have a residence visa, you must pay for your room in hard currency or credit card: hotels with ratings of two stars and up will not accept local currency

There are several four- and five-star hotels in Damascus: Sheraton; Dedeman Hotel (formerly Le Meridien); several units of the Cham (pronounced Sham), a Syrian chain; Fardoss Tower Hotel; Sahara Touristic Complex; and a brand new Four Seasons Hotel. The Omayyad Hotel is also decent and less expensive than those mentioned previously, but most of the others are dives—dirty and bug-infested. Only the one-star joints will accept Syrian currency.

Syrians

In the morning, you hit the streets to look over your surroundings. If you are in a conservative part of the city, you'll see women covered in black from head to toe—even in veils and gloves. You'll see men in caftans and various head wraps. You'll see some people dressed in casual western styles —blue jeans, T-shirts and Nikes. A peculiarly Damascene fashion for women is a plain white scarf tucked into a stylish raincoat—even in the blazing heat of summer! There are shops that specialise in these raincoats.

All these people will jostle you, run into you, and stare holes through you; a few may ask you in English, French or German where you're from. All the while, the traffic will besiege you with its din, pungent smells will invade your nostrils, and the exhaust fumes will choke you. But in summer, on the few quiet streets, you'll be delighted by the sound of cooing doves and the scent of pine and jasmine.

Street Safety

Be careful about crossing streets here. You must pay attention to the delicate choreography among vehicles and pedestrians. Pedestrians who hesitate, showing their intention to stop for oncoming vehicles then deciding to walk, might get hit. I was nudged by taxis twice during my first week. There seems to be no pedestrian right-of-way; vehicles won't stop for you unless you're actually in front of them. Also, cars often drive with their lights off at night so they can flash them at pedestrians and other drivers. The only two traffic rules I've been able to discern are: drive and walk offensively (the most aggressive driver or pedestrian wins the right-of-way); and whoever is in front has right-of-way, regardless of how he or she got there.

Narrow winding streets are a common feature that can be found in the old walled city of Damascus.

Also, there is little parking allowed on the streets, so cars are parked on most sidewalks, forcing pedestrians into the streets. As a pedestrian, you should be wary of many hazards other than traffic. For example, holes in the streets and sidewalks are usually unmarked—even at night; an Irish neighbour who was here with the UN fell into a hole and broke her ankle. Another danger is that pipes and trees are often chopped off a few inches above the surface at any point in the sidewalk. The third is that rubble from new construction and renovation lies everywhere and you might stumble over a chunk of masonry the size of your leg. Yet another hazard: the circular curbs protruding from many sidewalks enclose spaces for trees, but some of them have no trees and are therefore less conspicuous. A fifth danger is caused by low-hanging branches, wires and signs; I have even seen Syrians run into these hazards. Finally, the pavement tiles are often broken, missing or just very uneven. During daylight hours, it's easy enough to watch for all these things, but the problem is that at night only a few main thoroughfares are well lit.

Appearance

If you arrive in summer, the sunlight will be intense, white, burning. In winter, the wind could be biting, the sky and air gray. Regardless of the quality of light, you're likely to notice—if you are in tune to such things—that most of Damascus is not what one could call beautiful, even though it is captivating and has some visually redeeming qualities. This has not always been the case. In his three-volume series *The Venture of Islam: Conscience and History in a World Civilization*, Marshall G.S. Hodgson says (of the period from 1250 to 1503): "Some cities, such as Damascus... were especially famed for their beauty, (both) natural and artificial..."

First of all, the city is overwhelmingly brown, beige and tan, as is the mountain beside it (except in spring, when some greens and yellows pop up from the ground). Although the people and their dress are colourful, the height and density of the buildings are such that they overpower the splotches of colour with their drabness.

The majority of structures built since World War II are simply big square concrete boxes, stuccoed with what looks like unpainted mud and topped with forests of old TV antennas of every size and shape, leaning at all angles—although many of these are increasingly being replaced by satellite dishes. There is little architectural distinction here: one cannot usually differentiate an apartment building from a government office, an embassy, a school or an ambassador's residence. The city has a wealth of ancient structures, but sadly, most are in poor condition, many of them disintegrating. Those that are better kept are still drab and often dirty.

Another unsightly element is garbage. There aren't enough rubbish bins (and existing ones have no lids), so refuse in plastic bags is placed along curbs and sidewalks for daily pickup. The city's abundant wild cats feed on the food scraps, strewing the garbage everywhere. Most Syrians throw their trash everywhere. Many streets and sidewalks, despite almost daily cleaning, are scattered with waste of all kinds.

There are some aesthetic bright spots, however. One is the large number of trees and flowering shrubs in the newer parts of town. Jasmine is everywhere and scents the air on summer and autumn evenings. There are also a fair number of orange and fig trees, spicy-smelling pines, eucalyptus trees and various other sorts of greenery. Grapevines are abundant. The parks, too, are nicely designed and kept up, and show the vitality of city life on warm evenings—ponds, fountains, geese, ducks, children's playgrounds, flowers and paths. Unfortunately, most of the parks except the biggest one—Tishreen—have 'lawn police' who keep people from lounging on the grass: they want you to stay on the paths or benches.

An exception to the underwhelming architecture is in some of the mosques, a few historic buildings, and—in the newer areas of town where most foreigners and wealthy Damascenes live—new and recently renovated buildings. Most of this new construction and renovation is lovely, with golden-toned, hand-hewn stone exteriors. Also, decorative windows, doors, railings and columns are built from stone, nice woodwork or elaborate metalwork.

An example of the elaborate new architecture that Syrians seem to favour.

The newer mosques in particular are outstanding in their simple aesthetics and geometric designs. Their minarets have a unique Syrian design, those in neighbouring Islamic countries being noticeably different. An exception in embassy design is the embassy of the United Arab Emirates, a magnificent piece of neo-Arab architecture—the essence of graceful simplicity. And while the presidential palace (euphemistically named the People's Palace and built around 20 years ago on a hilltop overlooking the city) resembles a series of concrete boxes put together for a manufacturing plant, it can still be said that the Tishreen Palace is lovely.

DAMASCUS: OTHER CURIOSITIES

As you walk or cruise Damascus, there are other things that might strike you. One is that virtually every shop and office has at least one likeness—usually a photograph—of the late President Hafez al-Asad as well as the current President Bashar al-Asad displayed; some have several. In government buildings, every room will have one or more: for example, one small office area of the post office on Abu Romaneh Street has ten photos of the late president and nine of his son! This isn't always a sign of love, admiration or loyalty: it's expected. Their images on banners and statues can also be seen all over the city and throughout Syria, some statues dominating entire hills.

In 1994, when Hafez's eldest son Bassel al-Asad died, his images and photos outnumbered those of his father. Bassel's photos are displayed everywhere. Syrians seem to be mourning him still: Some will readily tell you about what a great man he was and how he genuinely cared about the Syrian people. With his dark aviator glasses and beret, Bassel looked a bit like the late South American revolutionary leader Ernesto 'Che' Guevara.

When I first arrived in Damascus in 1992, there was virtually nothing that resembled the commercialism of the West—no European, American or Japanese company names, no car dealerships, no junk food joints, nothing that even resembled a department store or supermarket, and no advertising billboards. It seemed to me like a different planet. In 1991, however, a new private investment law had just been instituted to liberalise private business, and things slowly began to change. Now there are some franchises such as KFC showing up, so can MacDonalds, Starbucks and 7-Eleven be far behind? The small shopkeeper, usually a family operation, is the standard here, and nearly all shops specialise in only a few items; there are even souks that specialise (see the section on Shopping in Chapter 6). The shops that are called 'Super Markets' are generally about the size of a convenience store in the United States and usually have less variety.

Something that may disturb you until you grow used to it is the military presence, although it seems a bit less overpowering now than it did under Hafez. Every government building, embassy, consulate, ambassador's residence, foreign school or cultural centre, and the homes of government officials have guard shacks out front and at least one soldier with an AK47; the more important ones have two or three soldiers as well as security people with pistols tucked in their belts. You simply cannot avoid the military presence in central Damascus, but except for occasionally making lewd remarks or noises at passing

women, they are non-threatening. I like to think of them as at least token protection from murderous religious and political factions. In reality, however, their ubiquitous presence owes as much to pragmatism—a way to use an idle army—as to anything else.

Another thing that will certainly catch your attention if you're unfamiliar with Mediterranean and Arab culture are the displays of physical affection among men. They not only hug and kiss each other's cheeks when greeting or saying goodbye, but some kiss each other's lips. Additionally, young boys, old white-haired men, and all ages in between walk around arm-in-arm or holding hands. Having grown up in the western United States where physical closeness among males usually comes either in fighting or homosexual contact, I was baffled by all this at first. I thought it was blatant homosexuality and was astonished that such a sexually repressive culture would tolerate it. Now I realise that you can simply take it at face value: men here are affectionate with each other, and they show it in the same manner they have for generations. And, it's far more pleasant than the macho posturing one sees in so many other places.

OVERVIEW OF LAND AND HISTORY

CHAPTER 2

'Every cultured man belongs to two nations:
his own and Syria.'
—from a Syrian tourist brochure

A GEOGRAPHY LESSON

Modern Syria (officially, the Syrian Arab Republic or SAR) was once part of a larger area that included what are now the countries of Syria, Jordan, Lebanon and Israel. This area has been called the Levant, Greater Syria and *Bilad ash-Sham* (the Arab name) and is still often referred to as the Levant.

The country of Syria is shaped somewhat like a triangle with irregular sides. You can drive from any border to any other in less than a day. Although it covers only 185,185 sq km (71,481 sq miles) Syria's strategic location has a historical

LADIES AND GENTLEMEN, SYRIA

importance to both Middle Eastern and Western civilisations far out of proportion to its size.

There are about 145 km (90 miles) of Mediterranean coastline and one island, called Arwad, just off the coast at Tartus. The island was an independent kingdom called Aradus in the days of the Phoenicians and contains many historical structures as well as a marina. Its inhabitants depend mostly on fishing for their livelihood.

Geography, vegetation and weather in Syria are quite varied. They range from mountains to steppes, from lushness to bareness and from moderate to extreme temperatures. Two-thirds of Syria is desert or steppe, as it is often called.

The western band of the country where most of the people live is less than 160 km (100 miles) wide and has a climate similar to other Mediterranean countries. Looking at it from the west, there is first a green coastal plain where temperatures range between 21–32°C (70–90°F) in summer and 10–21°C (50–70°F) in winter. It is always rather humid at the coast, where annual rainfall averages about 97 cm (38 inches). Beside the plain is a range of limestone mountains, which are cooler in summer and colder and often snow-covered in winter. Between this range and the next one is a drier but still fertile valley, called the Gharb Depression, which was a marsh in ancient times.

Next comes a range of dry mountains. The climate here is hotter in the summer and colder in the winter than in the western range. The narrow strip of land along the eastern slopes of this range is where the largest cities are, and the climate varies quite a bit from south to north. For example, the average rainfall in Aleppo (north) is about 47 cm (18.5 inches) per year, while it is only 23 cm (9 inches) in Damascus, farther south. The rainfall again increases near Jordan. The temperatures along this strip range from over 38°C (100°F) in summer to below freezing in winter.

The area east of the populated strip, with the exception of some mountainous land along the Turkish border and the irrigated land along the three main rivers, is high steppe and desert—not drifting sand dunes as in the Sahara, but rocky land. The Syrian Desert covers most of Jordan, Iraq and northern Saudi Arabia as well. It is different from North American deserts, which support a profusion of life. There is little vegetation other than sparse clumps of short grass in the late winter and early spring and the greenery in a few oases. The grass of the desert and steppes, however, supports Bedouin sheep and goats as it has for millennia.

The triangle of land northeast of the Euphrates and Al Khabur Rivers is called *al Jazeera* (island in Arabic) and is not as dry as the central desert, getting about 25 cm (10 inches) of annual rainfall. While most of the central desert is 762 metres (2,500 feet) or more above sea level, the Jazeera's elevation is around 366 metres (1,200 feet). This was once part of ancient Mesopotamia.

The desert in south-central Syria is an ancient volcanic area, covered by rough lava flows and dotted with cinder cones. Some of this land has been painstakingly cleared of lava rock so it can be used for agriculture.

According to many older residents in Damascus, the weather has been changing. According to them, in the 1980s, the summers were rarely hot for more than a few days at a time. But the winters of 1991–1992 and 1992–1993 were the worst in half a century, and the summer of 1993 saw more than three consecutive months of daytime temperatures above 35°C (95°F). Recent summer temperatures have also been quite hot, most likely as a result of global warming.

Syria has several rivers: the Euphrates, the Al Balikh, the Al Khabur, the Barada and the Orontes. The latter is the only north-flowing river in Syria, travelling through Turkey on its way to the Mediterranean. The coastal mountains have numerous small streams, some of which flow only during winter and spring, and the southwestern portion of the country also has small streams.

Syria has only two natural lakes. The biggest of these is Arram, which fills the crater of an extinct volcano in the Golan Heights. The other is Lake Mzerib, northeast of Der'a, near the border with Jordan. The country's largest body of water is Lake al-Asad, formed by the Tabaqah Dam on the Euphrates near Aleppo. Other lakes (all formed by dams) are Qattina, Al Rastan, Karma, Baloran and Karn. Until a few decades ago, the Barada filled two lakes east of Damascus. Now the river is completely consumed for drinking water and irrigation.

There are a few oases, the biggest and best known is in Tadmor, by the ruins of the Roman city of Palmyra. This was the source of life for that ancient city.

THE POPULATION

Syria's population has grown dramatically. At the end of the Ottoman empire it was about 200,000; in 1972, there were about 4.5 million people; in 1993, more than 13 million; as of 2000, there were about 17 million; and the CIA World Factbook estimate for 2010 was almost 22.2 million. This makes it one of the fastest growing countries in the world and one that is quickly running out of housing, water and places to grow food. Damascus, the capital, has grown from around 300,000 inhabitants a few decades ago to about 2 million in 1993 and as much as 3.5–4 million as of 2007 (for some reason, reliable figures for individual city/district population are hard to come by).

As of 2010, an estimated 35.8 per cent of the population was under 15 years of age, while only about 3.7 per cent was over 65 years of age—truly a culture of youth. As is the case

all over the Middle East and North Africa, population growth is straining the fragile ecology and economy of the area with pollution, garbage, crowding and demand for nonexistent jobs and water.

Despite these and other problems, Syrians are notorious for their friendliness and hospitality, and they seem to particularly like North Americans. They are almost manic socialisers and quite hyperactive, especially the young. They seem to like extreme things: foods that are either extremely sweet or sour, lots of jewellery, highly decorated houses, bright clothing, glitzy cars and lots of noise. Music and food form the main part of their social activities.

HISTORY

Syria has a rich and diverse history. The coast and the Euphrates River area have remnants of civilisations from as long as 7,000 years ago. Some structures built by the Romans, early Arabs, Ottomans and French are still in use. Until around the 29th century before the present (BP) the area had two mostly separate histories: eastern and western. In this chapter we will give only the barest possible outline of Syria's immense and involved history.

ANCIENT HISTORY
The West

The first known settlers on the coast were groups who had just begun to evolve from hunters and gatherers to sedentary people. They used the flint and obsidian tools found in Ugarit, on the north Syrian coast. They also left some statues of fertility goddesses but no containers of any sort.

A thousand years or so later, settlers here began using soft primitive pottery. During the 4th and 5th millennium BP, ceramics in elegant shapes, painted with geometric designs, began to appear. Similar pottery has been found all across northern Syria. For the next 2,000 years, pottery technology improved, and during the third millennium BP, copper work came into existence.

The history of the area becomes a little clearer with the Canaanites, who moved onto the coastal plain and the seaward side of the coastal mountains of what is now Israel, Lebanon and Syria. These people were called Phoenician by the Greeks. This name simply referred to all the peoples of the area, although none of them called themselves by that name, being composed of many disparate tribes, as they were.

The Phoenicians were the first great seafarers of the Mediterranean, establishing colonies and trading with people all around the Aegean Sea. It was during their time that the already ancient settlement at Ugarit was given its name. The Phoenicians developed and improved iron tools, and had the first royalty that wore purple robes. The dye for the robes came from a mollusc unique to the Mediterranean shores of Syria. The first known kings were Niqmadou and Yaqaroum. During the 36th century BP, the Egyptians invaded and conquered parts of Syria, but left the Canaanite kingdom intact; the two groups were friendly.

The earliest known writing in this area has its source in the reign of Niqmadou II (about 3360–3330 BP). The writing, using a cuneiform alphabet, tells a great deal about the customs and institutions of the coastal people. Clay tablets discovered at Ugarit and at Ebla, south of Aleppo, show that the Canaanite kingdom included a large chunk of what is now northwestern Syria, and speak of extensive diplomatic activity to safeguard the kingdom from the advance of both the Egyptians and the Hittites, invaders from the north. Eventually, war and political intrigue became increasingly common among the peoples at this end of the Mediterranean, and Ugarit was finally destroyed around the end of the 34th century BP. The city never rose again, but during the 26th and 25th centuries BP, Greek fishermen built dwellings atop the tell (a mound concealing one or more ancient settlements) and named the place Leukos Limen.

Around the end of the 34th century BP, about the same time as the Israelite migration into Phoenicia, another Semitic people known as the Aramaeans settled east of the coastal mountains. Their kingdom became known as Aram and eventually covered a large part of what is now Syria. From their capital in Damascus, they developed extensive overland trade with Asia.

The Aramaeans adapted the Phoenician alphabet for use with their own language, Aramaic, which eventually became the official language of the Persian empire. This is the language Christ spoke, and it is still spoken today in and around Maalula. It is also used in the liturgy of the Syrian Orthodox Church.

Aram prospered for hundreds of years, and completes the separate history of western Syria.

Maalula, a mostly Christian village north of Damascus. There is both a monastery and a convent here, and the Syrian Orthodox Church, which uses the ancient Aramaic langauge in its liturgy, began here.

Visitors at a cave chapel at Maalula.

The East

At the same time the Phoenicians were thriving, the ancient Sumerians (of what is now southern Iraq) spread northwestward into what is now eastern Syria and northern Iraq, eventually occupying most of the land between and around the Euphrates and Tigris Rivers. The area is often referred to as Mesopotamia, the Fertile Crescent and Babylonia. The people became known as Babylonians. Mari, an archaeological site on the Euphrates River near Iraq, has turned up evidence of settlers as far back as those in Ugarit —7,000 years ago.

While the Babylonians spread throughout the Fertile Crescent, the Assyrian civilisation was developing on the northern Tigris River. The Assyrians, from which Syria got its name, were as well known for their military conquests and brutality as the Babylonians were for their accomplishments in science, the arts and religion.

In the 45th century BP a group of Semitic people under a leader known as Sargon conquered Babylonia and established a kingdom called Akkad. A short time later, Akkad fell to Guti barbarians from the Zagros mountains (between modern Turkey and Iran). In the 40th century BP, Amorites conquered the region. Then the Assyrians took over Babylonia in the 35th century. By 3300 BP, they had occupied most of what is now Syria. In the 31st century BP, the Aramaeans drove them back, reclaiming most of their former empire.

Common History

In the 29th century BP, the Assyrians returned and conquered all of Syria, ending the separate historical development. This empire did not last long, though: in the 28th century BP, the area was conquered by the Babylonians under King Nebuchadnezzar. A hundred years later, Syria became part of the Persian empire. Then, in 2333 BP, Alexander the Great conquered it and it remained a Hellenistic outpost until it became part of the Roman empire in the 22nd century BP.

It took time for the Romans to establish themselves throughout Syria, but once they did, it became a major part of the Eastern Roman (Byzantine) empire for hundreds of

Halebiyeh on the Euphrates River marked the easternmost outpost during Roman times.

years. Of all Syria's conquerors, the Romans left the largest number of remains: cities, amphitheatres, temples and forts throughout the country. Three Roman emperors came from Syria. The best-known was perhaps Philip (1763–1758 BP). His birthplace of Shahba, south of Damascus, has ruins of a Roman theatre and baths and a museum of well-preserved mosaic floors. The other two emperors came from Homs (called Emesa at that time), 160 km (100 miles) north of Damascus: Alexander (Lucius) Severus (1814–1796 BP), and Elagabalus (1789–1785 BP).

HISTORY UNDER ISLAM

After Prophet Mohammed's death, his followers were divided over who should lead them. The Shi'ites argued that it had to be a family member of the prophet, and chose Ali, his nephew. The majority of followers, the Sunnis, wanted to appoint Caliphs to rule in his place. Immediate animosity developed between the two groups and continues today, although now the disputes are as much political, social and economic as they are religious. In addition to the split between the Shi'ites and Sunnis, there were conflicts between clans struggling for political and religious power.

The Omayyads were initially the strongest of these clans and ruled the Arab empire from Syria, between the mid-28th and mid-29th centuries BP. They were less dogmatic than other Muslim groups and more socially and politically oriented. Then, as now, the main opponents of Arab rulers were those who considered themselves pious Muslims fighting secularisation: these people wanted Islamic principles to be encoded as the law of the land. They were predominantly Shi'ites from what is now southern Iraq and Persia (Iran). If you would like to hear a case of repeated history, there's this: in *The Venture of Islam: Conscience and History in a World Civilisation*, the author states that the Persians, impressed with their own piety, passed a death sentence upon the Omayyads and others they thought were heretics!

The Omayyads left their mark in the lovely Omayyad Mosque in Damascus. This was built 1,400 years ago and incorporates ruins of the Cathedral of St. John, which in turn was built over the remains of a Roman temple. The mosque is one of the oldest in the world and is still in use. It contains a sepulchre that Muslims believe holds the head of John the Baptist.

The conflict between the Omayyads and other groups was not only religious; it was also between rural and urban power. Under the Omayyads, for the first time in the Middle East, political administration, education, intellectual pursuits and other aspects of city life were more highly valued than was rural life. The continuing conflict between rural and urban, Sunni and Shi'ite, and the clans finally overpowered the Omayyads around the middle of the 8th century. The Babylonians conquered the area then and intentionally neglected the coastal area, which fell under Egypt's control.

From 900–1,000 years ago, Greater Syria developed many local principalities and emirates, and this political fragmentation allowed the invading French Crusaders to take over much of northern and western Syria. The Crusaders came in waves, building mighty hilltop fortresses that still stand. Part of the battle here was for Jerusalem—one of the holiest cities in Christianity, Islam and Judaism. Eight hundred years later, the battle still rages, politically and otherwise, for control of Jerusalem.

Despite their success on the coast and in the mountains, the Crusaders had little impact on central and eastern Syria. Near the end of the 8th century BP, the last of them were expelled by the famous Saladin (Salah al-Din, in Arabic) and by the Mamluks from Egypt, who then colonised Syria.

Approximately 200 years later, the Turkish Ottomans conquered the area and have probably had the strongest influence on modern Syria. For one thing, they brought a certain amount of material success to the land. For another, they were Sunni Muslims like most Syrians. They also allowed local administration by Arabs who were at least nominally loyal to them. These administrators were wealthy landowners with deep roots in cities such as Damascus and Aleppo.

The Ottomans ruled until the end of World War I, about 400 years, which brings us to the turbulent 20th century. In order to understand the conflicts in this area, it is important to know a little about the background of the conflicting factions.

20TH CENTURY HISTORY

Christian groups have always played a prominent role in Syria, especially in the mountainous west and north. When the Meccans (Muslim Omayyads) first arrived, they stayed in the lowlands and deserts where the climate was more like home. Various Christian groups, perhaps fearing persecution from the Muslims as well as conflicts with other Christians, moved farther into the mountains, forming separate communities. In later years, minority sects of Islam did the same: Alawites in northern Syria, Druze in southern Syria and Lebanon, Shi'ites in what is now southern Lebanon. Under the Mamluks, non-Muslim groups were given some autonomy. The Ottomans expanded the autonomy, creating what was called the Millet system: Jewish and Christian communities had their own governments within the empire.

The French Mandate

The Syrian connection with France is important for several reasons. First, there were the French Crusaders. Then, as far back as the mid-16th century, the Ottomans had given the French commercial privileges in Syria. These were known as Capitulations and increased as time went by; they included the French as protectors of the Levant's Roman Catholic communities and the Russians as protectors of Greek Orthodox communities.

After the Turks were driven out of Syria in World War I, France and England bargained hard with each other for the spoils. It was a case of absolute political, religious and economic self-interest. This, combined with ignorance of the cultures involved, allowed Greater Syria to be chopped into pieces with little consideration for social or religious commonalities within the new countries.

Lebanon was proclaimed a "country" in 1920. This land, which had been a significant part of Greater Syria for thousands of years and which contained a multitude of religious communities, had little to recommend it for statehood. But the French wanted to protect the Maronites (Roman Catholics who practise Eastern Orthodox rites), who were in the majority there at that time. No consideration was apparently given to the potential for devastating conflicts in the new country. Thomas Friedman, in his book *From Beirut to Jerusalem*, compared the Maronites' Phalangist political and military party to the Roman Catholic Mafioso in Italy. The Muslim groups, particularly the Shi'ites, grew faster than the Christian population and began to resent the minority Christian domination. Then, Palestinians, who were driven out of their homeland by the Zionists, moved into the fray, using southern Lebanon as a base to fight the government of Israel. The rest is bloody modern history.

Modern Syria also has a fragmented population, but not as badly fragmented as that of Lebanon. It has a clear majority of Sunni Muslims, and the proportion of various groups has remained stable over the years. There are Kurds concentrated in the northeast, Armenians in the north and northwest, a few Shi'ites in the south, Alawites in the northwest, and Druze in the southwest. There are a few Jews, mostly in Damascus and Aleppo, and a few predominantly Christian communities—most notably Maalula (the ancient village north of Damascus where Aramaic is still spoken) and Armenian villages along the northwestern border with Turkey.

The Sykes-Picot Agreement of May 1916 divided the Levant between Britain and France, and Syria and Lebanon went to France. Iraq (including what is now Kuwait), Transjordan and Palestine went to Great Britain. The Balfour Declaration (British) of 1917 promised the European Jews a homeland in Palestine without regard for the Arabs who had lived there for millennia.

Despite the fact that the League of Nations didn't approve this partition until 1923, France took over Syria and Lebanon in 1920. The League mandate promised both countries a constitution within three years and stated that these documents be formed in consultation with local leaders and with agreement of the countries' citizens. Yet Lebanon's constitution was created in Paris and implemented in 1926 with no local consultations. Syria did not have a constitution until 1930. When the elected Syrian Constitutional Assembly prepared a draft constitution, French authorities objected to several articles, including one that called for the reuniting of Syria, Jordan, Palestine and Lebanon. When the Assembly refused to change the articles, the French High Commissioner dissolved the body, then later implemented the constitution with the articles annulled.

Another French violation of the mandate came in, allowing Turkey to annex the lush northwestern corner of Syria (called the Alexandretta and also the Hatay Peninsula) in 1938.

The essence of the mandate's weakness is summed up by Professor Ziadeh in Syria and Lebanon (1968) as follows: "The mandate gave France complete domination over Syria and Lebanon's foreign affairs, judiciary system, economic life and development and supervision of education and social welfare. The spirit of the mandate system put France under obligation to 'train' the people in these matters, but the mandatory power instead regarded Syria and Lebanon as an area of exploitation, where French capital, French colonial expansion, and French culture should be developed. The interests of the people themselves were a matter of secondary importance."

Syria rebelled against French rule during 1925–1927, but was crushed by superior military power, including a French bombardment of Damascus.

Things came to a head again during World War II. The Vichy government of France allowed the Germans to use airfields in Syria, en route to Iraq. Since the British were in Iraq, this caused fighting on Syrian soil between French and British forces, as well as between British and German forces. Germany had political designs on the Levant (mostly to drive the British out of Iraq, which made the Germans popular with the Arabs), and as the war drew on, the Soviet Union and the United States began to question what should happen in the Middle East. Negotiations were held, treaties were signed and the British took control of most French positions in Syria.

Then in June of 1945, Article 78 was adopted by the new United Nations. It stated that members of the organisation could not be placed under the trusteeship of another. On 7 June that year, the Arab League declared that the French and British forces in the Levant violated their countries' independence and sovereignty, based on the UN article. Britain protested that it was only there to maintain the new countries' independence, but both the United States and the Soviet Union declared that neither France nor Britain should be there. (In fact, the United States had recommended that Syria be made a constitutional monarchy after World War I, a suggestion rejected by Britain and France.) Finally, after a lot of wrangling and hostilities, French troops left Syria on 17 April 1946, and Lebanon on 31 December the same year. In Syria, 17 April is observed as Evacuation Day, a national holiday celebrated with fireworks, parades and other special events.

Independence

When a country—a collection of disparate cultures, really—achieves independence for the first time, it faces overwhelming problems, and the new countries of the Levant had more than they could handle. One was that part of geographic Syria had been given away by the Americans and British to Europeans—the Zionist Jews of Europe. Moving in next door to the new Muslim Arab states were people whose explicit goal was to take back the Holy Land from the Arabs. There was almost immediate fighting, as anyone with knowledge of the area might have foreseen.

Also, the economies were weak. While Lebanon had been both developed and plundered by the French, Syria had only been plundered. Few roads or railroads were built under the French mandate, and the remaining land and its climate made most of the new state of Syria unable to support a lot of human habitation. Despite millennia of being part of advanced empires, Syria was still mostly pastoral.

These difficulties and others resulted in a series of military coups from the beginning of independence. Pan-Arabism (the belief that all Arab people should be part of one nation-state), an idealistic concept to most Arabs since the 19th century, found an outlet in the union of Syria and Egypt in 1958. The new country was called the United Arab Republic. But Egypt's much larger population, military strength and Gamal Abdul Nasser's force of personality completely dominated Syria; the union lasted only until 1961, when Syria reestablished an independent government. Then in the mid-1960s a group of dissident military officers came to power through the growing and powerful Ba'ath Party, a Pan-Arab party in Syria and Iraq. This coup ended hundreds of years of domination by outsiders and—during the last few centuries—the Sunni landowners loyal to them: the new military officers were peasants from minority sects, and the Ba'ath Party itself was strongly socialistic.

From the beginning of independence, socialism appealed to many Syrians. For one thing, Islam appeals to the lower strata of society in part because it is egalitarian; the religion has no hierarchy. For another, many were tired of the aristocrats who had cooperated with the Ottomans for centuries, enhancing their own wealth and power. The Ba'ath Party was founded by two men—one Christian and one Muslim. In the newly formed nationalism, the uniting factor was not religion but being an oppressed Arab. The socialist nature of the new party shows in its founding congress statement (1947) that "The Arab woman enjoys all the rights of citizenship. The party struggles to raise up woman's level..." This was a truly radical concept in Arab culture, which for thousands of years had considered women as little more than the property, servants and sexual playthings of men.

The country's new leader was too dogmatic for Hafez al-Asad, the Minister of Defence, who had a more pragmatic approach to politics. In 1970, he and troops loyal to him (mostly from his clan and religious group, the Alawites) surrounded Parliament and took over the country in a bloodless coup. He held power until his death in 2000.

THE GOVERNMENT AND BA'ATH PARTY

In 1971, Mr Hafez al-Asad (*asad* means lion in Arabic) was elected president by an assembly of his choosing, and launched what is called the Correctionist Movement. This movement claimed that al-Asad's immediate predecessor, Salah Jadid—a fellow Alawite whom al-Asad had helped put into power, had erred in his unbending support for communist-type collective farms, an economy run completely by the national government and support for the Palestinian struggle in Israel at the expense of Syria's own wellbeing. The Correctionist Movement was to 'correct' these mistakes.

On 10 June 2000, Hafez al-Asad died after holding power over Syria for three decades. He was given a lavish state funeral. His son, Dr Bashar al-Asad, an ophthalmologist, was promptly named the country's new president. Just 36 years old when appointed, he remains popular with many Syrians for his progressive views, which he balances with a strong sense of Syrian pride and tradition. The President received his higher education in the United Kingdom and probably owes his contemporary views about government and his country's role in the world at least in part to this Western education.

During his first year in office, Bashar made several sweeping changes, including the release of hundreds of

political prisoners and allowing political parties (other than the Ba'ath Party) to publish. He also tolerated—for a time, anyway—a group of democracy advocate intellectuals' request for political and economic change, which is something his father would not have done. Traditions die hard, though, and in a country where there are powerfully entrenched military, bureaucratic and secret police forces, changes occur slowly. For example, soon after his appointment, Bashar made many liberalising moves, creating what is now called the 'Damascus Spring'. Emboldened and given hope by the new atmosphere, democratisation and liberalisation advocates began operating openly, and several were elected to the National Assembly, where they pushed for a more democratic society with civil rights. The democratic movement gained momentum rapidly, obviously scaring the government, and Riad Saif and nine other activists were arrested and jailed for several years by a conservative backlash. Four of the defendants were just released in January of 2007, several months before the official completion of their sentences, and Mr Saif—a member of Parliament at the time of his arrest—has become a powerful emblem for those who wish to see democracy in Syria.

In an interview with Kevin Sites of *In the Hot Zone*, he had this to say: "Before prison we were very tolerant of the regime, maybe too tolerant, maybe even a little naïve. We thought, 'Mr. Asad is this civilised man, this doctor—we have to help him move Syria from an authoritarian regime to a democracy as he will seek equal rights for everyone'." He says he no longer believes that, yet he believes the government will now allow him to continue operating as he did before. Why? "They are forced to," he says. "Otherwise what is the cost of putting Riad Saif in prison? If they take me to prison again then I'll be a real hero." In other words, the momentum seems to have been set, and only a massive, brutal repression—something very unlikely to happen—could kill it.

Government Structure

Syria's present constitution was established in 1973, and gives the president almost total control of the country. Ostensibly, his term of office is seven years. The Ba'ath Party is essentially an organ of the government and is committed to indoctrinating the country's youth about the glory of the Party and the 'wise and historic leadership' of President Hafez al-Asad and his successor.

The government is composed of several bodies and offices. A prime minister and a cabinet of around three dozen members (the number varies from time to time) are appointed solely by the president. The People's Assembly debates laws and directives proposed by the government, discusses cabinet programmes, approves the nation's budget and approves the nomination from the Ba'ath party of the president. It also has the power to override presidential vetoes by a two-thirds vote, but that has never happened —perhaps for the same reason that no one has ever run against the president (according to official government statistics, Hafez received 99.9 per cent of the vote in 1991). The Assembly, however, is the closest thing the country has to a democratic institution. All adult citizens can vote, and one-third of the candidates for the Assembly need not be from the Ba'ath Party. Quite a few of them are women. Although the constitution requires that the president be a Muslim, there are no religious qualifications for the Assembly. The constitution does require at least half the Assembly members to be workers and peasants. An Assembly term of office is four years.

In Spring 2007, during the national elections for the Assembly, Syrian cities were covered with posters and slogans of candidates; they were even plastered on the sides of the city buses. The candidates (2,000 of them for just over 200 seats!) gave speeches and shook hands all over the country. On the surface, it appeared to be similar to any election in any Western democracy and was described as being 'free and democratic' by the government and Ba'ath Party. However, opposition groups boycotted it, calling it a 'farce'. Why? For one thing, two-thirds of the members must be from the Ba'ath party; for another, the assembly can propose no laws and has no say in foreign policy; and perhaps most important of all, political dissidents who were jailed in the past can neither stand for office nor vote—although they were released from prison, they've been stripped of their civil rights. Of course, Bashar al-Asad has been nominated by the party for a second seven-year term (the only candidate from any party) and one of the first tasks of the new Assembly will be to approve his nomination. Although the election may be a farce to us Westerners, one can look at it this way: only a decade ago, it would have been unimaginable for the government to allow open opposition and to release political prisoners.

Local governments in Syria are divided into 13 provinces plus city administrations, but these are in all ways appendages of the national government. This sort of central control is common to countries of the Middle East. The Arab countries never developed the kind of semi-independent city and provincial governments that exist in Europe, despite the attempts of the Greek and Roman empires to establish that tradition.

Military

All young men are required to register for the draft when they turn 18. Then, at the age of 19, the conscription begins. There are only a couple of official ways out of this. One is that an only son cannot be drafted; another is for the young men who leave Syria to work in the Persian Gulf (it is called the Arabian Gulf here), earning up to ten times the salary they would in Syria. These are allowed to skip the draft by payment of a 'fee' which can range up to the equivalent of US$ 5,000. And of course, in a land where wealth and power has many privileges not available to those less fortunate, that wealth and power can "buy" a son's way out of the mandatory service, even though it's not an official policy.

Syria has an army, an air force and a small navy, which is only a defensive coast guard. It also has the presidential guard, which is under the command of a member of al-Asad's family and is a separate force.

Young women may also volunteer for military service, although not for combat. There are separate training academies for female cadets.

The Ba'ath Party

The Party (officially called Ba'ath Arab Socialist Party) is headed by a 21-person Regional Command—also, of course, chaired by President al-Asad. There are many organisations under the Regional Command: the Revolutionary Youth Organisation; the Union of Students; the Women's Organisation; the Peasants' Federation; the General Federation of Trade Unions; groups for journalists, electrical engineers and just about every other pursuit. The army, with its draft system, is a source of indoctrination through a special military branch of the Party.

THE ECONOMY

Reliable figures about the Syrian economy are less hard to come by than they were in the past. However, official government data is still questionable as it often does not match that of the World Bank, the IMF and other international economic organisations. Also, the government—despite recent attempts to become more open—is autocratic and secretive. Despite this, general information from the past is historical fact, and a fairly clear picture is emerging of Syria's current economic direction.

Under the new leadership, Syria's economy is undergoing

a slow but sure transformation for the better. Several changes enacted in the private sector, for example, have helped boost the economy. These include easier trading procedures, a wider availability of industry opportunities for private companies, simpler foreign exchanges, greater access to foreign markets and less government intervention in general. Additionally, more young Syrians are pursuing educations abroad and are returning better-equipped to deal in the new global economy.

Economic Changes

From the time of the coup in the mid-1960s until the mid-1980s, Syria's economy was highly centralised. All utilities, transportation systems and industries were owned and operated by the government. Small merchants, craftsmen, professional people, farmers, shepherds and landlords were free to operate their own means of livelihood, but with government-mandated price controls. Under al-Asad, farms were not collectivised and private property was not banned.

After the dissolution of the Soviet Union—Syria's longtime patron, Syria began to move away from its strong central economic control. Investment Law No. 10, a 1991 directive of the president's, liberalised economic restrictions and encouraged private investment in certain areas. The government, however, remained the country's banker and still remains its utilities and petroleum manager. The government also still heavily subsidises public transportation, sets prices on fuel as well as bread, lamb and other basic foods, and operates many heavy industries.

With the ever-increasing liberalisation of the economy, Syria appears to be following a development path similar to that of other countries such as China and Vietnam, in which many are becoming very rich and the middle class is growing, but many at the bottom social-economic levels are falling behind and becoming resentful of the wealth they see growing around them.

Since Syria has been and is still somewhat marginalised by the West—particularly the US, it has turned largely to Iran,

Turkey and other Arab countries for outside investments. Economic ties with Iran have never been stronger, epitomised perhaps by a new Iranian auto manufacturing plant (the first in Syria), a new public transport system to replace the aging mini-buses that have been in use for nearly 15 years, a new oil refinery and a joint bank. There is, however, some serious concern among many Syrians—including many in the government—about the side effects of this economic assistance and investment by Iran: namely, Iran's apparent attempt to increase the influence and number of Shi'a Muslims in the country. Many new Shi'a mosques have been built, and according to one government official, some Sunni Muslims have converted to Shi'ism. Even a group of religious scholars in Saudi Arabia has recently cautioned the Syrian government about the possible inroads of power Iran could gain in this way.

Despite the economic liberalisation, the government (bureaucracy, military, etc.) still consumes about three-quarters of the country's budget. However, the government has recently announced that it will not be recruiting new employees as it has in the past, so some attrition will be taking place in the near future.

Currency and Jobs

The unit of currency is the Syrian pound (SP), also sometimes called *lira*. It comes in paper denominations of 5, 10, 25, 50, 100 and 500 pounds and coins of 1 pound and 25 and 50 *piastres* (100 *piastres* per pound). The official currency exchange rate as of 2010 was around 47 SP per US dollar. The rate, however, has fluctuated over the past 15 years from a low of around 45 SP per US dollar in the early 1990s to as high as 58 SP in recent years. Many foreign residents take advantage of a black market, in which US dollars and other hard foreign currency are exchanged at a considerably higher value than the official.

With few exceptions, Syrians are able to pursue a variety of livelihoods. One exception is that only the top students are allowed into medical school, then the next highest level of students into engineering. Once a Syrian completes medical school, he or she most often continues studies and/or internships in the United States or Europe. Another exception is that an engineering graduate must work five years after graduation for the government (for about 3,500 SP per month) before going into private practice or working outside the country. In practice, however, family and social pressure as well as economic reality often dictate what career a young person pursues, despite the official freedom of choice.

Although the disparity between rich and poor is much less pronounced in Syria than it is in Egypt, Mexico or even the United States, most foreigners are baffled by how well so many Syrians live on unbelievably meagre salaries. The average monthly salary of most workers and professionals (without a private practice) range from around 1,500 SP for a janitor to 5,000 SP for a geologist who has been on the job for 30 years. This is the equivalent of about US$ 30–100. University professors fare only a little better, and even cabinet members' salaries are incredibly low by Western standards. Yet a modest two-bedroom apartment in Damascus costs several hundred US dollars a month to rent and the equivalent of US$ 100,000 or more to buy. So how do Syrians survive economically?

There are several ways. First, the government has rent control laws that help established families afford their living quarters; an apartment that could be rented to a foreigner for more than US$ 1,000 per month might cost a long-time Syrian tenant the equivalent of a few dollars per month. Then, families with money assist their children for most of their lives, or at least until the children earn enough.

Third, nearly everyone works at several jobs. An example: my best friend in Syria worked as an electrical engineer for the government in the morning, a European company in the early afternoon, then operated his video rental store until 9:00 pm or so. The routine is repeated every day except Friday—the official Syrian weekend. Millions of Syrians follow a similar pattern.

A fourth means of economic survival is black market activity. It sometimes seems like huge numbers of city people participate in unofficial currency exchanges and/or smuggling. Finally, families pool their incomes and young people rarely leave home before marriage. Some even live with parents for several years after marriage. With a little family inheritance, maybe a small shop and a half-dozen salaries, they survive.

Crops and Exports

Syria is self-sufficient in most basic foods. It produces a large amount of chicken and lamb and some beef. Its primary vegetables and fruits are chickpeas, lentils, tomatoes, potatoes, onions, cucumbers, cabbages, beans (both dried and green), squash, eggplants, artichokes, peas, corn, parsley, lettuce, melons, peaches, pears, apples, figs, dates, grapes, olives and pistachios. The southwestern area of the country near the Jordanian border might be called the nation's breadbasket, since this is where most of the wheat is grown. A new crop—tobacco—has been introduced into this fertile area to augment the wheat, melons, corn, prickly pears, pomegranates and abundance of grapes already produced here.

Some of Syria's abundant produce at a fruit and vegetable stand in the Friday market.

Syria's primary exports are oil, cotton (grown mostly around the Euphrates and in the north) and wheat. There are also a growing number of import-export businesses that export such things as food and industrial products and Syrian-made clothing.

GOVERNMENT SUPPORT VS. OPPOSITION
Class Conflict

Many wealthy Sunnis, especially those with generations-old roots in Aleppo and Damascus, think of the government people as peasants. In the 1960s, these established families lost their power, and new laws were established to aid the working class.

This conflict is noted in many books written about Syria, and I experienced it when invited for dinner one evening at the home of a wealthy older couple. These folks were world travellers whose large, elaborate home was filled with furniture, art, curtains and chandeliers from the United States, Europe and Southeast Asia. The woman was of Turkish descent, but had been born in Syria; the man was from an old Damascene family and had grown up in a classic Damascene home in the old walled city. Both are Sunni Muslims.

For a half hour, our host talked bitterly about the destruction of Damascus by the 'farmers' who were in charge of the government. He described how lovely Damascus had been when he was a child a half-century before: how clean the Barada River was, how safe and clean the city was and how everyone knew and trusted each other. Then he decried the mass movement into the city of farmers who were accustomed to the filth of the farm and brought it with them to the city; how the government's greed for income had overloaded the city with cars (tariffs on cars used to go up to 256 per cent; a Mercedes that cost an American US$ 60,000 cost a Syrian the equivalent of more than US$ 200,000 in the 1990s), destroying its peacefulness and requiring the elimination of many trees and flowers to broaden the streets; how the farmers and soldiers who ran the government had simply become a new class of aristocrats with their extravagant apartments and European luxury cars; and how anyone with political power could get away with anything: he could injure or kill someone in a traffic accident, for example, and the traffic police and civilian witnesses would be afraid to do anything about it.

The sad thing is, what this man said bears a lot of truth: I heard the same thing from other Syrians and saw some of it myself every day. There are many, many shiny new Mercedes and BMWs on the streets of Damascus. It's been said that the government, in return for loyalty, buys luxury cars for its top dogs, even though electricity is off for hours every day outside Damascus and government salaries are too low to even live modestly on.

Corruption

A second element feeding discontent with the government is corruption. Corruption in autocratic states is really no news; in Syria its brazenness can be shocking. It ranges from petty bribery such as paying a traffic cop to avoid a ticket to payoffs that allow big-time smuggling.

While driving on the Mediterranean coast with a Syrian friend, I asked him who owned an extravagant villa along the road. He replied, "A big-time smuggler." "How could someone be so openly successful in such a venture?" I asked, baffled. He said that since the government had little hard currency to buy imports, it tacitly allowed smuggling. Creative smugglers load donkeys with contraband in the mountains of Lebanon and send them across the border to Syria. In the 1990s, if one drove from the city of Homs to the Syrian coast, where the road parallels (and is only a short distance from) the northern border of Lebanon, sellers of contraband stood alongside the highway peddling their goods.

A taxi ride from Damascus to Amman in Jordan is an unusual experience for several reasons, but smuggling is a main attraction. Before leaving Damascus, the drivers might ask each passenger to take one carton of cigarettes (Jordan's entry limit) and may hide a dozen or so under the wheel wells, in seat-back chambers, under the seats, etc. Even though the Jordanian customs agents often tear incoming cars apart to search for contraband, they seem reluctant to inconvenience non-Arab visitors, so they are often less thorough in searching taxis with foreign passengers. On the return trip, the taxi driver might want some of your floor or seat space for a large bag of lemons or limes. At the border, the driver will hand a customs agent a wad of SP, sometimes in full view of the passengers, for allowing him to bring in the contraband. Cigarettes are much cheaper in Lebanon than in Jordan; lemons and limes are much cheaper in Jordan than in Syria.

Another form of corruption takes the form of blatant bureaucratic dishonesty. I knew Syrians who had ordered and paid for phone lines 10, 15, even, 18 years before and did not have them. Students told me about people who ordered and paid for cars 10 or more years ealier when they cost much less than in the 1990s, but still didn't have their cars. If they did receive their orders so many years later, they would have had to pay much more (tariffs had increased dramatically) or simply lose their original investments. The phone problem has been alleviated to some degree, though, by the use of cell phones, which are becoming increasingly common in Syria, and cars are now easier to import and have dramatically reduced import tariffs.

Religion and Bloody Rebellion

The strongest element of hatred for the government was at one time religious. Many Sunni Muslims thought the Alawites were heretics. It is a small sect, limited mostly to the coastal mountains of northern Syria, is very secretive, and is usually thought to be more Christian than Muslim, despite the fact that it is an ancient offshoot of Shi'ism. Although in the early 1990s there were many Sunnis in the inner circle of power, 10–15 years earlier both orthodox Sunnis and the radical fundamentalists were disgusted that secularists had taken over a country with 1,200 years of Islamic government. In Islam, government is not separated from any other part of life, but Syria's government under the Ba'ath Party is explicitly secular.

From 1976 to 1978, assassinations of government and Party people by Muslim extremists were aimed at the

Alawites and Iraqis (who were in Syria as part of the Pan-Arab Ba'ath Party) involved in the al-Asad government. After a brief respite the attacks began again in 1979 and escalated. Cadets at an artillery school in Aleppo were gunned down; the offices of Aeroflot Airlines were attacked; a Soviet diplomat was assassinated; and a car bomb near the centre of Damascus killed and injured dozens of people. The government was brutal in its attempt to put down the rebellion but was not successful until Hama.

In 1980, Hafez al-Asad was the target of an attack with machine-guns and grenades. A bodyguard was killed and the president was injured. Then the next year a bomb went off at the prime minister's office, killing nearly two dozen people. This called for war, and the president's younger brother, Rifaat, was in charge of it. The city of Hama, about 200 km (125 miles) north of Damascus, was a stronghold of fanatic fundamentalist Muslims (primarily the Sunni Muslim Brotherhood), so that's where the government hit.

Troops first attempted to ferret out the well-armed radicals, but were trapped and massacred. After nearly a month of these deadly raids, they went all out against the anti-government forces. Tanks encircled the city and blasted their way in, killing everyone in front of them and levelling much of the city. After the tanks withdrew, bulldozers came in and levelled the rubble, burying thousands of bodies along with it. When the rebuilding started, it was on top of the remains. The government made no attempt to hide the massacre, apparently hoping that knowledge of it would strongly discourage any other such challenge.

No one knows for sure how many people were killed, but Thomas Friedman, in his book *From Beirut to Jerusalem*, claims Rifaat boasted that 30,000 or more perished in the devastation. Despite the massacre, Friedman claims that even moderate opponents of al-Asad's background and policies felt that such action was better and less destructive in the long run than for Syria to become another Lebanon; the Lebanese civil war was raging at that very time and ravaged that country for more than a decade.

Repression

Syria has a terrible human rights record. Middle East Watch and Amnesty International both report that the country still has many political prisoners, and torture is common. In recent years the government has been trying to clean up its image and many political prisoners have been released. The government will now also tell the US Embassy whether or not a certain person is in prison and give the details of conviction, health status, etc. But there are still thousands in jail, many of whom have never had a trial. Those that get tried in the State Security Courts are doomed before the trial starts because they cannot consult with an attorney or their families and the courts do not operate in any internationally acceptable manner. While people are not usually hung or shot for opposing the government, torture is reported to be routine, and the condition of Syrian prisons is dreadful; it's quite common for prisoners who are not in good health to die while serving time.

Perhaps the worst part of the situation is that families are often not allowed to visit their relatives in prison. I know Syrians who have relatives that have been incarcerated for a dozen years, but no one in their families has ever seen them. The only information they get is secondhand, via other people who are able to visit family members in jail. In a culture where family is supreme, refusing family visitation is psychological torture.

The Positive Side

Most Syrians seem philosophical about their government, frequently joking about it. Also, recent changes, such as the new leadership of President Bashar al-Asad, appear to have made many Syrians feel happier as well as more secure and optimistic about their country's future.

The country has been stable for more than 25 years, and people seem to have a considerable amount of freedom, even when it comes to grumbling about the government. Jewish children can study Hebrew and Armenian children learn their ancestral language and their history, for example. These things were not allowed ten years ago.

The country also seems to have formed a sense of nationhood for the first time in its almost 50 years of independence. The majority of people have never known another government and have been indoctrinated in school, university, military and on the job by the Party. It also means that a unique culture has had time to gestate, particularly in the cities, where most people live. Many Syrians remember Lebanon and its devastation. They may have learned the value of compromise from that disaster.

UNCERTAINTY ABOUT THE FUTURE

Despite President Bashar al-Asad's early success and popularity, Syria's political future still remains somewhat uncertain. With the periodically escalating tension between Israel and Palestine, Syrian peace talks with Israel have also essentially come to a standstill. Bones of contention plague both sides. A few years ago, Israel threatened to attack Syria and Lebanon if these countries did not handover the Lebanese Shi'ite Muslim guerrillas who took three Israelis prisoner in October 2000. Syria and Lebanon, on the other hand, are demanding a complete withdrawal of Israeli troops from the Golan Heights, a request that Israel continues to deny.

Then, in 2006, Israel attacked Lebanon, and the resulting turmoil engulfed Syria, as it supports the Hezbolla fighters who provoked the attack. Recently, however, both Syria and Israel have said they are ready to intiate peace talks again.

The lopsided success of the economy could also be a problem. A handful of people are becoming wealthy while most others suffer: rents have climbed dramatically and general inflation is increasing while wages have not even kept pace with prices, much less given the average Syrian a better life. There also seems to be some resentment toward the newly wealthy, who are usually in favour with the government and love extravagant displays of wealth and prestige. Luxury cars are everywhere while most people cannot afford a car at all.

PEOPLE

CHAPTER 3

'All mankind is divided into three classes:
those that are immovable, those that are moveable,
and those that move.'
—Arab proverb

THE SYRIANS

One who has no good for his family has no good for any other.

Marriage is fate and destiny. (Meaning: It is not necessary to marry the one you love.)

Halime returned to her old habit. (Human beings can't change themselves, and if they try they will fail.)

Throughout its lifetime, the tree never reached its God. (Don't be too ambitious; be content with what God has provided.)

What has been written on the forehead, the eye will see. (What has been ordained by God will happen sooner or later.)

Whoever marries my mother will be my stepfather. (I will obey and respect anyone who has higher status or is more powerful than me, no matter who he is.)

Feed the mouth, the eye will be shy. (If you tip someone, he will not hinder your business.)

—Old Arab proverbs

At least two things make Syria a truly special place in which to live. One is the abundance of deserted historical and archaeological sites; the other is the people.

Syrians seem to be a bundle of contradictions, making them simultaneously fascinating and frustrating. While they are verbally polite, they have no qualms about pushing in front of you in line, jostling you so that you drop what you're trying to carry, or terrorising pedestrians when they drive; while some taxi drivers and shopkeepers offer you goods and services gratis as a welcome, a lot of others cannot be trusted for a minute; while most Syrians go out of their way to be hospitable, they honk their horns incessantly, play blasting music, and talk in loud voices outside your bedroom window at midnight or 6 am; and the same man who might surreptitiously fondle a non-Arab woman in a crowded souk will usually be polite and helpful if a woman asks for help or directions.

Syria's unique blend of civilisations and empires has produced a culture that seems not to be completely Arab (although most Syrians consider themselves Arab), not quite European (although the educated, urban Syrians seem more southern European than Arab), yet certainly not eastern Asian or African. With their long, rich history, their strong position in the Middle East, and a fairly high rate of literacy, Syrians think of themselves as the cream of the Arab world. They are proud, rarely beg, and are never obsequious. They generally scorn what they call the Gulfies—people from the oil-rich Arab countries—as nomads who lived in goatskin tents until they struck it rich through no effort or ability of their own, and whose cultural heritage is feeble compared to Syria's; they disdain Egyptians for being obsequious and (they claim) willing to do anything for money; and they generally think of most other north Africans as backward.

Despite these common attitudes, they show no arrogance or condescension toward most Westerners, and they make extra effort to welcome and help visitors from the West. Strangers often asked me if I was French, English, German, Spanish or Russian; when I told them I was American, they usually responded with a warm welcome and wanted to know what I was doing there, how I liked Syria, whether or not I had children, etc. When I responded positively about the hospitality of Syria, their faces lit up. They are proud of that characteristic.

It is not uncommon for a shopkeeper to close up his or her shop (there are a few women-operated shops) and walk you several blocks to show you where you can have a key made or buy a fan. Also, if you present shopkeepers with larger currency than they have change for or if you don't have enough cash for your purchase, they're likely to give you the item you want and say, *"Bukra, ma'alish"* (tomorrow, no problem). This is true even if they've never seen you before. When you do return to pay them, they act so pleased. My former partner bought a pair of gold earrings and was short about 4,000 Syrian pounds (about US$ 80). The shopkeeper said, "That's OK. Go ahead and take them and bring the money next week."

SOCIAL INTENSITY

One thing a visitor to Syria notices quickly is the energy put into personal relationships. It's obvious on the streets and in homes, schools and offices. When Syrian friends greet each other, their hellos and goodbyes take a while. They ask about each other's families—work, school and health—and where are you going and when are you going to come visit us? Then they say goodbye several times with various blessings on each other. When they learn English, these habits come through in the new language, and they'll ask you how you are two or three consecutive times. If you wish to endear yourself to Syrians, learn and use the expressions they use, even if you don't speak much Arabic. Even a surly government employee or taxi driver often becomes cordial if you greet him with the right expressions.

To stand on a street corner or sit in a park and watch the energy put into social intercourse can be both entertaining and enlightening for people from cultures that lack such an attribute. If you've spent time in other Mediterranean cultures, you'll see similarities here.

Personal Space

Along with social intensity comes the physical closeness described in Chapter One: embracing, kissing and holding arms or hands among the same genders. Syrian friends touch each other constantly. Even engaged young lovers and older married people sometimes walk arm-in-arm or hand-in-hand, although this isn't nearly as common as physical contact between the same genders. The concept of husband and wife as best friends seems to be a foreign one.

This culture of closeness causes discomfort for some expatriates from places such as the United States and northern Europe, where personal space is revered. If you walk the streets and souks of Syria, you are allowed no personal space. Suppose you're walking down a nearly deserted sidewalk three metres wide while a Syrian is walking toward you. Not wanting to crowd, you veer off to one side to give both parties plenty of space. The Syrian will often veer *toward* you and may actually brush up against you. No malice or challenge is involved; young women, old men and children all do it. It appears to be pure force of habit, an apparent desire to be close to people. In fact, if you are a woman walking through a crowded souk, a local female who recognises that you are a foreigner might even gently grab your elbow and guide you through the dizzying maze of people—even though she is a complete stranger. Once you get used to this affinity for smaller personal space, it is really quite nice at times.

A student once told me an old Arab proverb: "Where there are no people, there is hell." Syrians, with few exceptions, do not like to be alone and my students couldn't comprehend why I enjoy hiking in wilderness areas away from people.

Staring

This is another aspect of intensity that bothers many foreigners (especially women). In this culture, it is not a challenge for one man to stare at another as it might be in some other cultures. Nor is it considered rude for men on the street to stare at a woman, even if she's with another man. It is often the intensity and duration of the look that is upsetting. The peculiar thing is, if you stare back, the 'offender' won't look away and may actually start up a conversation.

The farther a non-Arab visitor travels from the centre of Damascus, where most foreigners live, the more he or she is the object of intense scrutiny. Along the Euphrates River, for example, rental cars are noticed a half kilometre away, and everyone near the road—in cars, on foot, on a donkey or working the fields—becomes your audience. You might hear whistles or greetings or questions called out to you. To walk down the street in Deir ez-Zor or Palmyra is to feel as if you are the main attraction in some kind of freak show. This was true for both my Black and Chinese friends as well. If you

A child in the village of Bursa stares curiously at the photographer.

spend much time in a shop, natives will gather around the door to look, some of them trying to talk to you in their often limited English, French or German. Foreign women, as one might expect in a macho culture, receive the most attention from men, but also a lot from Syrian women.

Personal Questions

Another lack of personal space is less tangible. The Syrians are terribly curious about foreigners and ask a lot of personal questions. They don't understand if you are reluctant to answer them, particularly questions about families. For a woman to tell a Syrian that she doesn't want to get married or to have children is to see a look of incomprehension. For a man to admit he's had a vasectomy elicits the same response. To tell them that your college-age children live alone back in your hometown is baffling to them.

ATTITUDES ABOUT LIFE

Syrians love to laugh and joke, eat and talk and dance. They love noise—loud music, hand clapping, car horns, loud voices—and few of them I've discussed this with like peace and quiet at all. The younger ones have a tremendous amount of energy, even when in their mid-20s; to spend a day on an outing with young Syrians is exhausting.

The Role of Fate

A fatalistic sense of humour comes through clearly in Syrian political comments, which mostly take the form of jokes. I heard many al-Asad (Hafez) jokes, and rumour had it that he even enjoyed some of them.

In this culture, fate is everything, and is reflected in the constant use of *insha'allah*, which roughly means if Allah wills it, whenever talking about the future. Many Arabist scholars have noted the determinism of Islam, and reading the Koran confirms it. This 'culture of fate' shows up in various ways. One is that time is not monitored and schedules are not adhered to as they are in the time-manic United States or Japan. Being on time does not matter because whatever is going to happen is going to happen anyway! I like this characteristic when I have a time commitment, but it's not so pleasant when I'm the one waiting.

Don't Try to Compete with Allah!

Things made in Syria simply don't work most of the time, and when they're repaired, they don't stay repaired. There seems to be limited commitment to quality workmanship and even less to excellence. This is even true of most handicrafts. You can buy a beautiful handmade brass teapot, for example, but not be able to use it because it won't pour straight or it leaks; you can buy gorgeous clothing, but it will show its age very quickly; carpenters and stone masons create lovely and elegant arches and woodwork, but the doors and windows are likely not to work well and you might pull electrical outlets from the wall when you unplug appliances; a painter will spend days meticulously painting plaster scrollwork on a ceiling, but leave windows covered with paint runs and wide swaths of brush marks. When you buy a bottle of fresh-squeezed *fuwaakee* (a blend of strawberry or raspberry, apple, banana and orange juices), the juice-shop boys will make sure the container is filled to the brim, but it'll likely be full of stems, seeds and too much pulp.

Some Syrians and expats I've discussed this with lay the blame on decades of socialism with guaranteed incomes and make-work jobs from the government. This may be a consideration, but I think it's a minor one. While the I'm-going-to-get-paid-no-matter-what attitude exists in some sectors of the economy, Syrians are generally hardworking people, seemingly without much taste for Western levels of comfort. There is almost no drunkenness (an apparent problem in many former communist countries; certainly a problem in Western countries) and most Syrians work at two or three jobs to survive. I think the cause lies in a Muslim ideal that striving for excellence is sin, because only Allah is perfect. While living there I did a great deal of shopping for local products and noticed quite clearly that the quality of the handicrafts made by Muslims generally was not as good as those made by Christians or Jews.

My Experience with Syrian Quality

Here's a first-hand illustration of Syrian quality: When living in my first apartment in Damascus, the braided hose from the water heater sprung a leak, so I called the rental agent who immediately sent his son over to repair it. The guy looked at the broken hose and told me that he had replaced it only a few months before. He said it was made in Syria, and that was typical of Syrian quality. He left and returned with a hose that looked for all the world like the one he was replacing, but he told me it was made in Germany, cost several times as much as the comparable Syrian hose, but would last much longer with no problems.

FAMILY ORIENTATION

Families are the centre of life in Syria, and this orientation shows up in many ways. One of the first questions a foreigner gets asked is "Are you married?" Another is "Do you have children?" If the answer to both questions is "Yes," the Syrian will want to know all about your family. If your children are unmarried and younger than their mid-20s, Syrians will usually be shocked if you left them in your home country. People there can't fathom children leaving home at the tender ages of 18, 19 or 20 (unless, of course, they are married), and they often make clear their belief that they are better parents than most Westerners. They point to things such as drug use, teenage pregnancy and suicide, and street kids as evidence that this is so. I've found that many young people cannot imagine leaving home when they're teenagers. Some of them complain about lack of privacy and about family pressures but generally seem to think it's for the wellbeing of everyone. And putting ageing parents in a nursing home (there are none in Syria) is anathema to them.

Getting married and having children is usually life's top priority. Children are so important (especially sons) that fathers and mothers traditionally change their names after the first son is born. Suppose they name the son Yassar: the father becomes Abu Yassar—literally father of Yassar—and the mother often becomes Umm Yassar—mother of Yassar. If no sons are born, the mother usually identifies herself as the mother of the firstborn daughter; fathers rarely do this, however.

Schoolchildren in Tartus. Having children is a Syrian's top priority.

Family orientation is more than just tradition, though. While there is some child abuse and children are punished harshly at times, I noticed a lot of affection displayed between siblings and between children and parents.

Deaths in the Family

When someone dies, there are three days of mourning during which time friends, relatives and neighbours visit the family. In Muslim homes, the family is expected to feed all these people. Close women relatives wear black for months after the death. After this period of time, they can start wearing black and white. For very traditional families, it may be a year or longer before the women can wear colours again; I had a friend whose mother had died nearly two years earlier, and she had only just begun to add a little colour to her still mostly black attire. For less traditional families, the mourning time is still at least several months.

If an older woman's husband dies and she is unlikely to remarry, she may wear black for the rest of her life. These traditions are similar in both Christian and Muslim families. A woman who does not fulfil certain minimum mourning traditions is criticised for not having loved the deceased. Of course, there are no such expectations of men.

When a Muslim dies, neither embalming nor cremation is allowed, so the person is buried within hours, without clothes and wrapped in a shroud, but can be buried only during daylight hours. Christian and Jewish families follow their own traditions for death.

The Darker Side of Family

These are mostly positive factors about families, but there are negative elements as well, which most Syrians don't admit to but which sometimes showed up in my students' journals.

One problem is unhealthy control of family members by a domineering father or a frustrated mother who can wield power only over her children. Many times young people who are deeply in love are refused their families' permission to marry because of a difference in social class or just because the mother of one dislikes the loved one. I became friends with an American woman (whose father was Egyptian) and a Syrian man whose mother wanted him to marry a particular Syrian woman. The man's mother made life so miserable for the couple that the young woman returned to the United States while the man stayed in Syria to work in his father's business. Few children, no matter how old, will defy their parents' wishes.

Another negative side—and this is more serious—is the tremendous population growth caused by a family-is-all-that-matters attitude. If creating your own family is the main reason for existence, and if manhood and motherhood are proven through producing lots of children, then the more children you have the

A fellow teacher received a journal from a female student who said she wanted only to die. She wanted to study in France, but her conservative father refused to even consider it. After his death she felt a ray of hope, only to have it quashed by her oldest brother who, according to tradition, took over control of the family and also refused to approve her request.

better. Syria and other countries of the Middle East have some of the highest birth rates in the world in a land that is mostly desert, and the problems caused by this growth are obvious in daily life: water and electricity shortages, shortage of living quarters despite new construction everywhere, rising prices, and severe pollution.

Many educated Syrians see the problem, but most still want to have three or four children, if only they could afford it.

GROUP THINKING

Syrians generally do not like to stand out from the crowd. First of all, they are clannish: immediate family first, then clan or village (sometimes these are about the same), religion next, and only then the individual. The variety in modes of dress might belie this conformity at a glance, but it is really part of it: they dress like their group.

There are many manifestations of this uniformity. One is that few Syrians are either fat or skinny. Another is that they dislike confrontations or scenes, especially with foreigners. I've seen a customs officer, a traffic cop or just a guy on the street back down when confronted by an angry Western woman with a loud voice. My former wife and I walked past groups of soldiers guarding an entrance to a building who made 'kissey' noises or muffled sexual comments. When I stopped, turned around and yelled *Shu?* ("What?" in Arabic), they invariably backed down and said something like, "Oh, hello," or just acted chastised.

Another group-think characteristic that becomes obvious is the attitude about food. Most Syrians simply do not like anything but their own cuisine, and it shows in the restaurants: they are overwhelmingly Syrian, and those that describe themselves as French, Italian, etc. are mostly poor imitations. If it isn't hommus, flat bread and kabob, it isn't real food to them, it seems. See Chapter 6 for more on Syrian food preferences, which can be a problem when you invite them to dine with you at your home.

Yet another result of group-think is the general lack of creativity in the lives of Syrians. Although there are a few artists and galleries, the work was a bit too uniform for me, a bit too much influenced by older European or American work. Islam's ban on representational art has left an artistic vacuum compared to the West or to Eastern Asia, I think. Syrian artisans make some truly beautiful handicrafts, but the patterns, designs and colours are mostly geometric and set by tradition. Mosque design and classical Arabic calligraphy are also beautiful, but without innovation, as a rule. (One notable exception to this is in the clothing made in Syria. It has an amazing profusion of colours, designs and motifs.)

Perhaps the most obvious sign of tradition over creativity is in naming children. Nearly every Muslim family in Syria that has a son names that son Mohammed. This is done not only out of respect for the Prophet, but because it's felt that it brings good fortune to the family and the son. Many Mohammeds use their middle names for a little distinction. Perhaps as many as three quarters of the Syrian men are named Mohammed, Ahmad, Khaldoun, Khaled, Yassar, Imad, Samer or one of a half-dozen other common names.

Who's Mohammed?

I've had classes in which half the males were Mohammed or three of them were Ahmad or Samer. There seems to be slightly more variation in female names, though.

My perception was that strong group mentality, combined with social intensity, also keeps most Syrians from being reflective. The picture I got from my students was that deep thinking, asking the big questions about life, even reading and writing, are less important than being socially oriented, keeping up appearances and sticking with tradition. This obviously hasn't always been the case because the Arabs of early Islam excelled in the sciences, math and other intellectual areas—even in art.

Some modern Arab scholars lament their people's enslavement to tradition at the expense of innovative and creative thinking. They also criticise the sentiment that only a return to what is perceived as the grand and glorious days of early Islam will find solutions to all of life's problems.

OTHER CHARACTERISTICS
Here are some other Syrian characteristics I noticed.

Mode of Dress
It would be difficult to find greater variation in dress than in Syria. Being a blend of cultures as it is, having every sect of Islam, both Eastern and Western Christianity, and disparate tribes from one corner of the country to the other, the clothing is often a treat for the eyes. A young woman wearing a white scarf and a raincoat walks down the street with her best friend—another young woman in tight blue jeans, with booming hair, heavy makeup and loads of jewellery. A father in caftan and *kafeeyeh* (a wrapped cotton headdress) might be walking along with his sons who are in blue jeans and T-shirts printed with English expressions on the front. A grandmother covered in black from head to foot might be with her granddaughter who's wearing colourful Syrian fashions and earrings the size of small chandeliers. On the other hand, many wealthy and educated Syrians dress similarly to Europeans or Americans. To add to this mix, every village and tribe of Bedouins seems to have its own particular patterns, styles and colours of clothing.

One item that perhaps symbolises not only Middle Eastern dress, but Muslim dress in general, is the head wrap; and in Syria, there is an endless variety of materials, colours, textures, patterns and styles of wrapping for both men and women. They range from elegant and gorgeous to torn, dirty or sun-bleached.

Middle- and upper-class Syrian women, especially the younger ones, tend to wear long hair in a quite fancy manner—usually permed. Conversely, the young men almost always have closely-cropped hair, but are also very dressy. Few of them wear blue jeans and running shoes, for example.

Some things you will rarely see in Syria: bare legs above the calf, bare shoulders or upper arms, shorts on adults (men or women), miniskirts, short hair on women and girls and long hair or earrings on men.

Physical Characteristics

Although most Syrians have light brown skin, dark brown eyes and black hair, there is surprising variety in physical attributes. They range from blonde hair and a pearly complexion to a dark chocolate skin colour and jet black hair. Quite a few Syrians have blue or pale gray eyes, although these usually have dark hair—I've only met a couple who have both blonde hair and blue eyes. Red hair and light brown hair is also common, sometimes accompanied by pale, freckled skin but brown eyes.

As is the case in most countries that have mixed colour, the lightest-skinned people dominate the top socio-economic positions and the dark-skinned people the lower ones. Government officials, business owners and models used in TV commercials are almost uniformly light-skinned and often European in appearance, while construction workers, janitors, garbage haulers and street cleaners are predominantly dark-skinned.

I think Syrians—especially the younger ones—are among the most physically beautiful people in the world, with soft, rounded facial features, gentle eyes and beautiful hair and

A Syrian man entertaining his friends at a picnic.

skin tone. There is a distinct Syrian look, although I can't quite pin it down. For example, I could usually distinguish a Syrian from other Arabs, particularly those from North Africa or the Gulf countries.

Political and Sexual Innocence

In part because the autocratic government has kept tight control of the citizens, Syrians seem politically naive by Western standards. Few of them have travelled outside the country. Most news has traditionally been either spoonfed by the government-owned news agency or reviewed and censored in the form of international newsmagazines and newspapers. Until recently, there have been few foreigners in the country—tourism is barely developed (a blessing, if you compare it to Egypt, for example) and there are still a limited number of foreign businesses with a noticeable presence in Syria. Damascus has more than 40 embassies, but most foreigners in the capital live in only a few areas of the city. All of these things create a social and moral atmosphere that somewhat echoes the United States during the 1950s, I felt.

Gender segregation and lack of dating creates sexual naivete—and powerful sexual preoccupation. Men aged 25 to 30 giggle over words like butt, panties and bra or over dirty jokes that are tame by present-day standards in the West. Grown men here often behave sexually like pre-adolescents in the United States.

An exception to this innocence, however, is the sense of government distrust among the population. Although things seem to have opened up compared to the Hafez era, still, no one knows for sure who works for the Mukhabarat (the secret police), so people are cautious about criticising the government to other Syrians they do not know well. This seems to be less true now than in the past, though, and many Syrians openly express their opinions to foreigners they trust.

Cynicism as we know it in the West is conspicuously absent. People here seem to have no taste for the sardonic. They expect little good from their governments and they usually get it. In Western democracies, on the other hand, it seems many of us expect *everything* from our governments and are endlessly disillusioned.

A bird and egg souk; birds are about the only household pet Syrians like.

Pets

Syrians generally do not seem fond of animals. Although a few people have pet cats and dogs, the house creatures of choice are caged songbirds. In warm weather the cages spend most of their time outside on balconies. Many shops also have songbirds. The birds create delightful bits of melody around parts of the cities.

At the same time, Syria has a serious problem with wild cats, which feed on the ubiquitous garbage. These pathetic, scruffy creatures are everywhere and are generally reviled by the locals, who kick or throw rocks at them.

Not Wanting to Disappoint

Suppose you ask for directions to go someplace. It seems that few natives will just say they don't know; they want to help you and be hospitable. So they're as likely as not to give you inadequate or wrong directions. I was on a trip to a monastery in the desert with a group of students, and the driver of the van did not know the way. In the town nearest the monastery he asked for directions three different times before we were finally guided in the right direction, this time by someone who hopped into the van with us to show us the way!

Another form of this peculiarity is that when you ask shopkeepers if they have a certain product or maybe some empty cartons, they will frequently say, "Maybe tomorrow"—even if they don't know for sure when they'll have what you want.

RELIGIOSITY

Although Syria has a large assortment of religious groups, most of them share a strong belief in God and a heavy religious influence in their lives. Muslim, Christian or Jew, Syrians' greetings, goodbyes and many other common expressions refer to God, thank Him for everything and leave the future up to divine providence.

The most common response when you ask someone how he or she is, is *al Hamdulla* which literally means, Thank Allah! The chapter about language gives several greetings and goodbyes in Arabic that mention God, and even when they speak another language, Syrians translate these into the new language: God bless you, God-willing, Thank God, God be with you, etc. Although I suspect that some of this is tradition without real feeling, I can hardly imagine people (other than a few fundamentalist Christians) in the West using similar expressions. Religion is part of everyday life here, and it seems most people wear their beliefs proudly and with no self-consciousness.

Approximately 10 per cent of Syria's population is Christian, primarily Syrian and Armenian Orthodox. There are a few Roman Catholics and even fewer Protestants. Only a few hundred Jews remain.

The remainder of the population is Muslim, and about 82 per cent of that is Sunni Muslim. Most of the 16 per cent that is not Sunni is Alawite or Druze—groups that have branched off from mainstream Islam. There are also a relative handful of Shi'ites and Ismailis. All of these groups seem to live together in relative harmony, although I sometimes detected somewhat hostile feelings among some groups while I was living there.

Islam means submission to Allah. Muslims believe that the religion is not a new one but a continuation of Judaism and Christianity with Mohammed being the last of the prophets and the Koran (the Islam holy book) superseding all other revelations from God. In the Koran, Muslims, Jews and Christians are all referred to as 'Children of The Book'.

Unlike Christianity, where virtually all sects have an official, universal leader (the Pope, for example), Islam has none. Each mosque has its holy man—called a sheikh—who holds his position as spiritual guide and Friday lecturer by virtue of his study of Islam and his perceived piety.

The Koran and the teachings of and examples set by the Prophet guide every aspect of Muslim life. Everything from government and commerce to daily routines are covered. The most prominent religious principles, called the Five Pillars of Islam, are as follows:

1. *Shahada* :The declaration that there is only one God and that Mohammed was his last prophet.
2. *Salat*: Prayer five times daily—at sunrise, midday, afternoon, sunset and evening. Prayers are prescribed in both form and content.

3. *Zakat*: An annual tithe of two and a half per cent of earnings above basic necessities. This money is used to build and maintain mosques and help the poor.

4. *Sawm*: Fasting during Ramadan, the ninth month of the Islamic year. During the fast, most Muslims do not eat, drink (even water), smoke, or have sex from before dawn until after sunset. It begins and ends—according to the instructions of the Koran—when one cannot distinguish a white thread from a black thread in natural light. The *sawm* also allows those who are travelling during Ramadan to fast at some other time. The purposes of the fast are to purify the soul and body and focus one's attention on God. In Syrian cities, the beginning and end of the fast are marked by cannons firing.

5. *Hajj*: The pilgrimage to Mecca, with a stop in Medina to pay respects at the Prophet's grave. This is required at least once in a lifetime, but only if the person has the financial means to do so. Some Muslims make the pilgrimage many times, and others pay for poorer friends and relatives to make the trip. The official time for the *hajj* is during days seven to ten of the 12th month of the Islamic year.

Islam is a complete guide for living. Some examples:

- No alcohol or illegal drugs are to be used.
- Men and women who are not members of the same family are forbidden to touch each other.
- A woman receives half the amount of inheritance a man receives.
- In a dispute or court, the testimony of two women equals that of one man.
- Muslims are supposed to eat with the right hand.
- The left hand is to be used for bathroom functions, which in the days of the Prophet meant wiping oneself with a handful of sand; thus the rule about eating with the right hand.
- A man must squat as a woman does to urinate.
- Muslim can neither be embalmed nor cremated and is buried naked except for a shroud.

Line Cutting

One Syrian behaviour that I found extremely irritating is the refusal of most Syrians to queue up and wait their turn. Line-cutting is the rule, and the intruders ignore even the most reviling comments from the few people who wait in an orderly fashion. Sometimes the guards (when there's a semblance of a queue, there are usually guards) will shoo the violators back from the front of the line—the favourite place to cut in—but the persistent ones simply sidle in a little way back, pretending they were there before and are only returning to their rightful spots. You can combat the line-cutters by simply refusing to allow them to crowd in front of you; of course, they may just go farther ahead and find someone who won't stop them from cutting in.

Lack of Environmental Consciousness

One of the most disturbing habits prevalent in Syria is the handling of garbage. Syrians, educated and uneducated, rich and poor alike, drop their waste everywhere.

While most homes are spotlessly clean and educated people are often quite self-conscious about their personal appearance, the streets and sidewalks are a mess. You see freshly scrubbed and meticulously dressed people walking down the street eating corn on the cob or ice cream from plastic dishes or drinking a can of soda. When they finish, they pitch the refuse aside with no self-awareness at all. Add this behaviour to that of the wild cats strewing garbage everywhere, and you can see the problem.

Everywhere you travel in Syria, even in the farthest reaches of the desert mountains, you will see garbage stuck in the ground, under rocks or on bushes. Farmers plough the ground and multi-coloured bags look like exotic flowers when viewed from a distance.

Maybe millennia of surviving the harshness of the desert has bred contempt, rather than appreciation, for nature. I've encountered few Syrians who have such appreciation, even

Wherever the Mediterranean coast is not cleaned daily, there's a mess of plastic refuse, dirty diapers, paper plates, you name it. The locals lie around on the beaches among the trash, seemingly oblivious to it and drop their own wherever it lands.

though the better educated ones are beginning to see a connection between the environment and the support of life. I've never heard a Syrian comment about the awe and beauty of a magnificent sunset or raging winter storm; they seem mostly oblivious to such things, focusing instead on people and social life.

While the government has the army planting trees throughout the country, the green belts around the major cities are being depleted by immense population growth, and surface water everywhere is undrinkable, unfit even for irrigation (but is used for it anyway, creating the intestinal problems mentioned elsewhere in this book). Mines and quarries in the deserts and mountains devastate large areas of topsoil, and the tailings are piled around the sites, creating thousands of hectares of dead and ugly land.

The Syrian ignorance of nature can be astounding. Students often asked me if I wasn't afraid of wolves and bears when I went hiking in the mountains. The only thing they can apparently equate genuine wildlife with is the vicious half-wild Bedouin dogs of the desert and the street cats of the cities.

A Nature's Tale

A fellow teacher once showed his class photos he had taken of an elk and some buffalo in Yellowstone Park (U.S.). The elk was nearly up against his car, and the students could not understand why he'd get so close to such a big, scary creature. The buffalo were shedding their winter coats, and one student asked why they looked ragged. The teacher explained about winter and summer coats on wildlife, how they needed the heavy fur and wool to survive the harsh winters but would shed it to be more fit for hot summer weather. The next question left the teacher momentarily speechless: the student asked how they took those coats off in the summer—did people help them do it? He was *not* joking.

Class and Racial Consciousness

As I mentioned before, there is social and economic discrimination between light- and dark-skinned people. While there is no violent racism in Syria as there is in the United States and Europe, I detected a general feeling of superiority among lighter-skinned Syrians. This comes through in comments and jokes. Blacks, particularly Africans, are not generally liked or respected, nor are the Bedouins, even though they are the original Arabs whose ancient cultural elements are still a big part of modern Arab life. Also, there are quite a few Sri Lankans and Indians there who work as servants, nannies and houseboys for foreigners and wealthy Syrians, and I often heard derogatory jokes about them among my students. It became clear to me that Caucasian Westerners receive friendlier treatment than do people who are darker-skinned.

Class consciousness is also very real. The neighbourhood they live in, whether they live on the top or bottom floor, what kind of car they drive (if any), and whether they wear Syrian or American and European fashions are all elements that place a Syrian in socioeconomic categories. It is often very difficult for young people who fall in love across these lines to marry each other, at least with family blessings.

It is not enough to have a lot of wealth; they must show it in the right ways to assure their acceptance into the class they aspire to. There is little socialising between upper and lower classes as there might be in Canada or the United States, and the lower socio-economic classes seem humble and accept their 'place'—perhaps the culture of fate again.

Manual labour of any kind is usually thought beneath the dignity of anyone in the upper classes. The rich do not spend time puttering around in the garden, doing repairs around the house or making things by hand, and wealthy Syrians have little desire to own any of the beautiful handicrafts made in Syria; they prefer something made by a machine in the United States or Europe, with a high price.

BEDOUINS AND VILLAGERS

No description of Arab people can be complete without discussing Bedouins—the original Arabs—and villagers.

Bedouins

Like indigenous people throughout the world, the Bedouins' traditional lifestyle has changed a great deal, and will probably disappear soon. This will not be the result of imperialism or colonialism as it has been with most other indigenous peoples, but from the encroachment of modern living with its intrusive electronics, transportation and commercialism. The people who are helping force them into modern civilisation are the city Arabs.

In *The Middle East* magazine, an elderly Bedouin was quoted as saying: "Fifty years ago there were no cars or trucks, only camels; ... people lived on barley, bread, dates, yogurt, *burghal* (bulgur) and dried pomegranate seed. We were living on the bounty of God. We were happy... I'd like an easier life, with a nice house, a warm bath, central heating and all; but in the city I wouldn't be able to afford more than a sandwich and a pack of cigarettes."

Another Bedouin talked about the difficulty of life as a desert nomad: "Bitter water. Dust. It's hot in summer, cold in winter. Scorpions. We have to go 20 km (12.4 miles) to find drinking water. What kind of life is this?"

Although those who still follow a nomadic life continue to live in the traditional black goatskin tents, other elements have changed irreversibly. If you travel through the desert and steppe during the spring when grazing is good there, you will see these tents everywhere; and parked beside most of them is not a camel, but a large sheep-hauling truck and maybe even a generator. Many tents have lights and television sets that run off either the generator or a truck battery. Children are often bused to school in a village.

Population growth and climate change have also contributed to the demise of traditional Bedouin life. Better health care has increased the life span at the same time that less land is fit for grazing or growing barley, and young Bedouins often end up in villages or cities where they farm or work at construction or street cleaning.

Despite the gradual elimination of the nomadic lifestyle, many elements of this ancient culture live on (if in modified form) in the daily lives of most Arabs: strict segregation of genders; arranged marriages; clannishness; submission to a strong and autocratic leader; belief in harsh punishments; a strict code of honour; and warm hospitality.

If you hike in the desert, Bedouins will often want to talk to you and may invite you to their tents for tea. The children sometimes beg, especially around population centres or places such as Palmyra where tourists regularly show up, but otherwise are just infinitely curious about foreigners. If you want to please the children (who tend sheep and goats even when they are quite young), bring pens and candy; they seem to want these most. If they ask for *bon bon* or *boom boom* they mean candy; if they ask for *qalam* or *alam* they mean a pen. One young boy tending his flock near the ruins in Palmyra walked a couple of kilometres to bring a lamb to me to hold and pet. I took his picture holding the lamb, then gave him a pen and 25 SP. He was elated.

Villagers

Although more and more people from villages are finishing high school and even attending college, basic village life in Syria hasn't changed a lot over the centuries. Villages don't have the wealth the cities do, there are relatively few cars, and ancient Arab cultural attributes are more noticeable than in the cities. These things are particularly true of desert villages and those along the Euphrates River.

Most Syrian villages have electricity, indoor plumbing, schools and clinics, but these things are not universal. Still, Syria's government has done a better job providing basic services to villages and rural people than governments have in many other developing countries.

The houses in the smallest villages are simple adobe-type huts of one or two rooms, while bigger villages and small cities also have a lot of apartment buildings. There are few camels in Syria. The most common work animal is the donkey, followed by the horse or mule.

FAMILIES AND WOMEN

Although Syrian women have a higher legal status than do their sisters in most other Arab countries, the attitudes and behavior that many men in Syria exhibit toward women is a fact that women and their families must deal with almost daily—thus the inclusion of women in the heading.

JOBS AND OTHER OPPORTUNITIES FOR SPOUSES

One of the stipulations of a Syrian visitor's visa is that you must not accept employment. The reality is, though, that various kinds of work are available.

IN SYRIA THE MAN'S THE BOSS,
IF THAT'S O.K. WITH YOU MY DOVE

Paid Employment

If you or your spouse have obtained work in Syria via an embassy, oil company or school, your whole family can get *iqaamas* (residence visas) through your employer's sponsorship. If you arrive without a job, your visitor's visa is good for six months. During this time, if you can get a job teaching in one of the foreign cultural centres (American, British, Spanish, French, German or Russian) or at an international school (American, French or Pakistani) or at a company, your employer can help you get *iqaamas*.

The American Language Centre and the British Council school teach English to adult Syrians, the French Cultural Centre teaches French and Arabic (the latter in French, of course), the Spanish centre gives Spanish lessons, the Russian centre teaches Russian, and the German (Goethe) centre teaches both German and Arabic (the latter in German, of course).

If you have a residence visa, you can accept just about any type of work available. For example, a fellow teacher who had worked as a graphic arts designer in the United States, did graphic design consulting for a company that produces business forms, cards and calendars.

The most flexible type of work is private language teaching. The demand for English tutors is strong, not only among Syrians, but among expats of other native language groups who want to improve or maintain their English proficiency. Native English speakers I know have tutored children of UN families, spouses of diplomats and even ambassadors. The going rate is around 400–800 Syrian pounds (US$ 8–15) per hour for an experienced tutor. This is as much as a local-hire teacher without a Master's degree currently gets paid at the American Language Centre or British Council school, and you don't have to attend meetings, create, revise or give tests, substitute for absent teachers and so on. Establishing the contacts necessary for tutoring takes time, but notices placed on bulletin boards at language schools, cultural centres and Syrian universities may soon bring more students than you can handle. The American Language Centre and British Council school also keep lists of tutors for referral.

Volunteerism

Aside from paid employment, there are opportunities for volunteer work in cultural centre libraries, various charities, archaeological excavations and historical restorations. These things take time to discover, and contacts with the international community will help you. Examples: the associations of American, British and Canadian women hold charity bazaars and the American Women of Damascus (AWD) has a library staffed by volunteers.

Educational Opportunities

There are several options for learning languages in Damascus. You can learn Spanish, French, German and Russian at their respective cultural centres, and you can find tutors for Italian, Turkish and other languages.

People who are fluent in Arabic can sign up for university classes, or just observe classes with permission from the professors or invitations from students. Some expats I knew took Arab history classes at the University of Damascus. Cultural centres and embassies (including the Arab Cultural Centre in Mezzeh) occasionally sponsor lectures from Arab and Fullbright scholars.

Drink vendor dressed in traditional attire.
These vendors roam the streets with their
water containers strapped to their back.

Rush hour traffic in Damascus. There are more cars in the city than the roads can handle, and it can be dangerous if you are not used to how the locals drive.

These waterwheels at Hama are known as Noria. They are 20 metres high and date back to the 13th century.

CHILDREN

There are many advantages to raising children in Syria: violent crime is rare in general and even rarer directed against children; illegal drugs are scarce; alcohol is not ubiquitous or easy for teenagers to get; and if you live in Damascus, the children will make friends from around the world and can learn several languages as they grow up. For these reasons, plus the fact that adults keep their eyes open to what goes on in their neighbourhoods, it's difficult for adolescents to get into serious trouble.

Education

One thing that is not a bargain is education for expat children. Although they can attend Syrian schools if they hold *iqaamas*, only one foreigner I knew has tried this and she found the quality of the schools unacceptable. This is to be expected in a system that still uses outdated educational methods and in which the teachers' monthly pay is about enough for a week's groceries. A further disadvantage is that although your children will learn Arabic with native fluency, they will not develop their own native language skills.

The alternatives to Syrian schools are mostly expensive. The Damascus Community School (DCS) seems to be the school of choice for both wealthy Syrians (about 45 per cent of the students are Syrian) and many diplomatic personnel. This is an American-accredited K-12 school with curriculum, activities and teaching methods similar to those in the United States. The drawback is cost: annual tuition at this time is over US$ 10,000 per student plus several hundred US dollars for testing and registration fees.

There are two other schools in which English is the language of instruction: the Pakistani International School and a private Syrian school called Rodaat Al Ashbaad. The Pakistani school has two campuses: for primary levels, near the Canadian Embassy in Mezzeh, and for secondary levels, near the Australian Embassy, also in Mezzeh. The annual cost is the equivalent of about US$ 3,000 per student. The Syrian school is located in a new village several kilometres outside Damascus, but buses shuttle the children to and from points near their homes. This school has a better reputation among expats than the Pakistani school. The annual tuition is equivalent to US$ 2,000 per student at this time, plus a small charge for bus transportation.

If you wish to have your children educated in a French system, the French school is located in the outskirts of Mezzeh. The costs vary depending on whether you are a citizen of France, Syria or another country. For families without French citizenship, the grade school costs 8,000 SP (US$ 160) per semester per student, and the high school about 21,000 SP (US$ 420) per student each semester. Parents I knew who sent their children there were impressed with the school.

One more option is to educate your children at home if someone in the family has the time, training, ability and inclination. Whether you do this or send them to school, you may be able to negotiate with your employer to cover educational expenses.

Parks, Playgrounds and Other Activities

Syrian cities—particularly Damascus—have many parks, and more vacant land is being turned into parks. Each park has a playground, and unlike some Western cities where you would never let children out of sight or even enter a park after dark, these are not concerns here. During hot summer nights, people hang around the parks until 11 pm or later, with children running free and having fun; elderly couples sit and chat; and young lovers steal a few minutes away from the prying eyes of society.

In addition to the amenities in public parks, Damascus Community School has a track, a gymnasium, a playground, a tennis court and a football field for the use of its students and teachers and their families, as well as for teachers at the American Language Centre and their families.

Syrian schoolchildren get out of school in the early afternoon and spend a great deal of time playing outdoors during good weather. As do children everywhere, they accept playmates from other countries with openness and curiosity.

Fortunately or unfortunately, depending on your viewpoint, teenagers have little Western-style entertainment here. The cinemas show mostly violent films—kick boxing and martial arts are Syrian favourites, and the people who attend are overwhelmingly young, lower-class males. There are few places to play billiards, few video game parlours or carnival-type rides, and bicycle riding can be deadly in the chaotic, high-speed traffic and narrow, crowded streets.

Shopping for Children

There are multitudes of stores that sell children's clothing, toys, and books in various languages (mostly Arabic, English and French). The clothing generally looks quite European or American but is less expensive than in the West. Some toy shops sell modern toys such as Lego, frisbees, etc., although the selection of Western toys and games is still a bit limited.

Child Care

Notices posted in the language schools, foreign cultural centres and embassies sometimes advertise for teenage children of expats or adult expat women who will babysit. Sri Lankan, Indian or Filipina nannies are inexpensive, and some can be hired for daytime duties only, others as live-ins.

MISCELLANEOUS

Here is other information that might be important to you.

Religious Activities

Although Syria is overwhelmingly Muslim, the tradition of Christianity is strong in the western part of the country: this is the land of Abraham, of St. Paul and other early Christians, and there have been stable and cohesive Christian groups from the begining. Freedom of religious expression is uninhibited, including for Jews, and there are numerous churches and synagogues in the western part of the country. Damascus, for example, has the historic St. Anthony's Roman Catholic Church (its bell tower stands only a few metres from the minaret of a mosque—a symbolic juxtaposition) near the Cham Palace Hotel. There is also a Roman Catholic church affiliated with and behind the Italian Hospital on Salheeyeh Street. Others include a Greek Catholic church on Abu

Romaneh Street, a Greek Orthodox church on Talay Al Foudda Street and the church of St. John beside the Swedish Embassy, just off Abu Romaneh Street. The latter has Protestant services as well as Anglican Catholic (Episcopalian) masses. There are also numerous smaller churches in the eastern part of the old walled city (the Baab Tooma and Baab Sharqee areas) as well as in the large neighbourhood north of Baab Touma.

Although few Jewish expats come to Syria, Damascus has more than 20 synagogues and Aleppo a dozen or so more. If you are Muslim, of course, you will find a mosque almost literally on every block.

Birth Control

The secular government of Syria encourages small families, unlike the government of Saudi Arabia, for example, which actively encourages large families.

There is a family planning agency in Damascus on Abu Romaneh Street, beside the Mercedes dealership and the Syria-Saudi Company. Birth control pills and information are available here. Also, most pharmacies sell condoms and other birth control devices.

FOREIGN WOMEN IN SYRIA

There are a few single Western women in the Middle East, but most women here are with families. All of them are guaranteed more attention than they want.

Dealing with Syrian Men

Anyone who has lived or travelled extensively around the Mediterranean or the Middle East is aware of the common attitudes and behaviours of the local men, particularly toward foreign women. In Syria, a foreign woman will simply never find indifference from most men or boys: their behaviour ranges from chivalrous to crude, depending on the circumstances and the person. While young men throughout the world whistle at, leer at, and make sexual comments to attractive young women, males here do not seem to discriminate much based on either age or appearance. The good news is that Syria is less this way than some other countries in the area.

Unwelcomed Looks

A Chinese friend who is now a citizen of Sweden and has lived most of her life in Europe described her anger at the leering way Syrian men look at her: "They look at me as if I'm cheap and that makes me angry—I'm not cheap." Another Swedish woman told of her time in Kuwait, how most Kuwaiti men would look away when she passed them on the street (a common reaction to foreign women in the rich Gulf countries). Thus, it was a real shock for her when she arrived in Syria and felt eyes burning through her.

For an older woman, the unwanted attention most often comes as intense staring and mumbled comments, often even when she is with a man. For young women, the attention is more ardent and includes leering, sexual comments and groping or unwelcome bodily contact.

Two things are baffling about this behaviour: it seems almost subconscious, habitual and unpremeditated; and even a woman 40–50 years old who the males find attractive is an object of rapt attention, often by boys young enough to be her grandchildren. I knew several middle-aged women who dressed conservatively, yet constantly suffered comments, kissing noises, and keen scrutiny from males ranging from grade school boys to men in their 30s: "Hello, come talk to me!" or "You're beautiful!" or "I love you, I love you!"

Syria has a great deal to offer the foreign observer, including the ancient walled city of Damascus (above), but women are advised to observe a few simple rules; dress conservatively, walk around in the day if alone and avoid crowded places.

The things that will bother you are not the looks or comments you don't understand but the kissing noises made at you, the comments you *do* understand and the fondling. Nearly every foreign woman I know who lives here has been groped. If someone does touch you in a sexual way, defend yourself: kick him in the groin, hit him and scream at him; not only will he usually slink away in humiliation, but someone is likely to come to your rescue. Groping women is not legal in Syria.

The examples of sexual harassment seem endless, but there is good news: rape is rare; the percentage of males who actually grope is small; many local men are both embarrassed by and apologetic about such behaviour and will come to your rescue; and there are ways a woman can protect herself. One is to avoid crowded places such as the souks unless you're with your husband or a male friend, and it's best if he walks behind you. Another is to ignore all comments, pretending the guys simply don't exist. A third is to avoid eye contact with all men you don't know well, again pretending they don't exist. Even in a shop, where the shopkeeper is unlikely to be friendly in an unacceptable way, it is best to be businesslike and brief in your exchanges. Finally, don't take taxis or walk around at night by yourself. These are things the Syrian women do for their own protection.

As infuriating as this behaviour is, it might help to understand its origins and causes. There have been volumes written about women in Arab and Islamic societies, and this is no treatise on the issue, but think of these facts. For more than 2,000 years Arab culture has considered women inferior to men, and often worthless as children. For hundreds of years before Islam, female children were routinely buried alive, women who gave birth to girls instead of boys were beaten, killed or—if they were lucky— just humiliated by their husbands and families.

Being Friendly

If you are a woman who is naturally gregarious and cordial, particularly with people who are friendly to you, you *must* break that habit with Syrian men; some will simply misinterpret your friendliness as either sexual looseness or possible romantic interest in them.

When Islam came along, it forbade these practices, but still relegated women to an inferior status, and the old ways died hard. The Koran states that men are superior to women because they are stronger (and for this reason are required to protect and support their families); that the testimony of *two* women is required to match that of *one* man (women are believed to be too emotional and too easily influenced); that women should receive only half as much inheritance as men (since, unlike men, they are not required to earn a living or support the family, and what women do bring to a marriage, or earn during one, belongs to them alone); that the servants of Allah will be served by and married to beautiful young virgins when they go to heaven; that, as a last resort a man may beat his wife if she disobeys him; and that a woman can have only one husband while a man can marry four women plus his slave girls, divorcing any of them at will.

Add this cultural and religious background to the socially enforced separation of men and women, and the male behaviour and lack of respect for women is not surprising. Most people are virgins until marriage, which is often at 25–30 years of age, and most social and any physical contact between young men and women considered normal in the West is not allowed. Basically, only the wealthy, westernised youth can find outlets—albeit secretly—for their hormonal impulses, and these sometimes include same-sex activities.

It is worth remembering that the Bible itself, in the writings of the misogynic St. Paul, considers women to be inferior, tells them to obey their husbands and not to speak in church. Also remember women's status in the United States and Europe less than a century ago and the binding of girls' feet in China. Syrian women today enjoy more freedom and respect than Western women did less than a century ago.

Dealing with Local Women

Now some good news. Syrian women love gossiping, but most of them are affectionate and friendly with foreign women. They are not only interested in your very different lives, but it is almost as if thousands of years of repression has created a sisterhood of protection and love. There are some exceptions to this, times when you may sense hostility from (usually) older and conservative women, but this is rare. Most Syrian women you have contact with will treat you almost as part of their families.

SOCIALISING WITH THE LOCALS

CHAPTER 4

'Have you heard the story of Abraham's honoured guests?
They went in to him and said "Peace!"
"Peace!" he answered and, seeing that they were strangers,
betook himself to his family and returned with a fatted calf.
He set it before them, saying: "Will you not eat?" '
—from the Koran

Hospitality in the Arab world is as old as Abraham. Visitors here are often surprised at the invitations they receive to visit the homes of Syrians they barely know or to have tea with a shopkeeper or a stranger in a village. This characteristic is not only religious in origin, but is ingrained in the Arab code of honour. Honour, in various forms, is critical to Arab people, and to be inhospitable, even to enemies, causes dishonour. In *The Arab Mind*, the author says hospitality "… is a noble trait, exhibited proudly even by the poorest Bedouin, and impressive even in the modified and reduced form in which one encounters it among Arab city folk."

AT A SYRIAN HOME
In stark contrast to the dirty and garbage-strewn streets, the interiors of most Syrian homes, especially of the middle and upper classes, are spotless. One rarely sees dust or fingerprints.

Styles and Furnishings
There really is not a typical Syrian home. The styles of decoration and furniture as well as the size of the home vary widely between social classes, Muslims and Christians, and traditional and modern attitudes. If there is a most common decor, however, it is the gaudy Louis XIV style. Despite the French presence here for so many years, you can't find a good cup of brewed coffee or decent bottle of local wine

anywhere; but in the 18th century French embellishment of furniture and architecture, the Syrians found something they could really latch onto. Ceilings tend to be high and sculpted with plaster, which is then sometimes painted in a variety of colours; elaborate wallpaper is common in older homes; furniture is highly decorated, upholstered with multi-coloured fabric and the wooden framework often gilded.

The chandeliers and other light fixtures are what truly stamp a place as Syrian. Many chandeliers are oversized for the rooms they light, sometimes hanging down to below head-level and, seen from the streets at night, often filling an entire window. The brass frames are smothered with multi-faceted glass that brings to mind the opulence of a French palace. Other lamps and light fixtures tend to be equally overpowering: brass floor lamps shaped like palm trees; table lamps glazed in pearlescent black or white with flowers, dolphins or other decorations in brass-covered relief. All of this ornateness usually rests on colourful French, Turkish or Persian carpets and multi-coloured stone floors.

Many of the newer houses and those recently renovated lean toward modern European styles, accented with some Syrian glitz. At the other end of the age spectrum lie the one-time grand houses of the old walled city. These are hundreds of years old, each built around a courtyard with a fountain and a private garden of grapevines, citrus, eucalyptus and other trees and flowers. The ceilings range between three and six meters (10 and 20 feet) high, the better to keep rooms cool during scorching summer days. Sadly, most of these have deteriorated badly and/or been chopped up into smaller houses or rental rooms.

Being a Good Guest

So you've been invited home for tea, lunch or dinner by a Syrian you don't know well. It is a faux pas to decline an invitation unless circumstances make it impossible to accept. And unless the invitation is clear, it would be wise to fish around for whether or not your spouse or children are also invited.

It is common and acceptable to arrive a little later than the specified time, except during Ramadan (the Islamic month of day-long fasting) when those who have fasted dive into their evening meals with a vengeance. Arrive a little early for dinner feasting during this month.

Do not bring food or drink as a gift for the hosts. Nothing is expected, but flowers are about the only acceptable gift. Don't be offended if they simply disappear—they're probably displayed in another part of the house.

The furniture is almost always arranged in a recognisable pattern, whether chairs, sofas or cushions on the floor: the perimeter of salons is filled with places to sit. This reflects the nature of Arab socialising, where everyone sits in a circle of talk.

In the more traditional homes, the women and girls sit more or less at one end while the men and boys sit at the other. If there is more than one salon, the genders may separate completely. In less traditional homes, there seems to be no definite seating pattern, although the guests usually sit together facing the hosts.

Bringing Gifts

Do not bring food or drink as a gift. Nothing is expected, but flowers are about the only acceptable gift. Don't be offended if they simply disappear—they're probably displayed in another part of the house.

Tea or coffee (and perhaps alcoholic beverages in a non-Muslim home) and hors d'oeuvres can last a long time. Then, if you're staying for a meal, don't expect to leave for about two hours at lunch, three hours or more at dinner. Meals, especially those eaten with friends or visitors, are a major source of social life and entertainment.

When the meal is served, the hosts usually tell you where to sit. While traditional Muslims do not eat with their left hand (the Koran says to use that one for toilet functions), few of the Syrians I knew would be offended if you used your left hand. It would be considerate to point out that you simply cannot do it with your right one. However, never use your left one to pass anything to others. The only other thing to remember is to eat slowly, because you will be pressured to eat and eat until everything on the table is gone—this is a tradition. If you simply can't, you must graciously say, "No, thank you" several times, or say *daeema*, to get your host to stop feeding you.

Let the hosts guide the conversation so as to avoid touchy subjects; they will always have many questions for you anyway. The hosts appreciate questions about their families: number of children and grandchildren, ages, where they live, and if they have relatives living abroad. But if your hosts are conservative Muslims, don't be too inquisitive about female members of the family. Inquiries about work (cautiously, though, if someone works for the government) are acceptable, as are general questions about Syria. Israel (still usually called Palestine) is a touchy subject. If the hosts bring it up, be cautious about your response, particularly if you aren't sure about their religious or political views. Your comments about the Syrian government should either be neutral or positive. If the wrong person perceives you as being harshly critical of the government, your visa and residency permit could be endangered.

OTHER SOCIALISING

An invitation to someone's home is the most common form of socialising, but you're likely also to be invited to lunch or dinner with a group. It's difficult to say no to an invitation:

Syrian university students making their favourite food—kabobs—at a picnic.

Syrians are quite persistent. If you must decline an invitation once or twice, you will probably have to accept the next one to avoid blatant rudeness. Do not expect to be invited to go to a play or movie, on a Sunday drive or to various other activities; in Syria a meal or tea/coffee and snack is nearly the sole form of socialising, except among young single people who just 'hang out' on Thursday evening or—if they're males —go to a movie with their peers.

Women commonly invite other women to tea, coffee or lunch and expect them to come alone; men do the same with other men. A couple of the men in one of my classes asked if I wanted to go out for dinner. In my naiveté I also assumed an invitation for my partner at that time, with the whole class going. The following day one of the men and one of the women in the class approached me and asked if my wife could come also, so my female students could come. They didn't want to miss out on the fun but apparently didn't plan on going unless my wife went. On the other hand, a class of younger students wanted to take me to a special place in the country for lunch. It was clear from the beginning that both males and females would be going. My wife couldn't make it, but I didn't let them know that. When I showed up alone, most of them were disappointed.

In Public Places

If you're invited to a party, there will usually be no alcohol, but there will be plenty of sweets, loud music, singing and dancing, and the men will be quite forceful in persuading their guests (male and female) to get up and dance. Despite the image most Westerners have of the erotic Arab belly dancer (a myth from *The Arabian Nights*) Arab women will not dance in front of men; the young men are the ones who get up and belly dance, sometimes even on table tops, imitating the breast-jiggling of real belly dancers. It's quite comic, and they relish it, laughing hysterically at each other. This is done in restaurants, on picnics, in the classroom, in the parks, and just about any other place they 'make a party'. There is a special lap-held drum that is commonly used outdoors in lieu of taped or live music. The dancing is also accompanied by fervent hand clapping and occasionally by the high-pitched voice and rapid tongue clicking that is an ancient vocal expression of Arab women.

Whatever invitation you receive, your hosts will refuse to accept a contribution for the food. It is futile to try to pay but shows politeness, anyway.

At Your Home

Most Syrians are accustomed to dropping in on friends and family unannounced, even late at night. Most seem to be sensitive about doing the same to foreigners, but it does happen. For this reason, I rarely let my students know where I lived. If you have contact with a lot of Syrians who know your phone number, many of them will call you at all hours, often inviting themselves over on a moment's notice. If you value your privacy and solitude at home—the only place you can find such things in this culture—you must perform a balancing act between showing politeness and appreciation for their good intentions and protecting your own emotional well-being.

You may wish to invite some Syrians to your home for dinner or lunch (breakfast is usually not a social event for Syrians). Most people eat lunch around 2 to 3 pm and dinner around 8 to 10 pm and socialise for several hours before, during and after the meal.

It is difficult to know what to serve your guests, so it would be a good idea to feel them out for what types of food they like or would be willing to try. Some may want to try Western-style home cooking, while others do not like much of anything but Syrian cuisine (or the Syrianised versions of such things as pizza, hot dogs and hamburgers), and you cannot compete with their own home versions of their own food. I have found Damascenes in particular to be extremely particular about their food. I've watched them pick around at a fresh roasted turkey or excellent lasagna as if they're trying to find something they can call food! I've heard students complain about the Syrian food at a restaurant in a rural area or village, saying that it doesn't have enough of this or that, and how much better Damascus' food is. The best advice I can give about cooking for Syrian guests is not to assume they will like something, even if you think it is succulent; don't be disappointed if they don't rave about it or want second helpings.

Dress

Syrians, for the most part, really dress up for social occasions. If you wear blue jeans and a T-shirt you will stand out. Whether you go out to lunch or dinner or to someone's home, you will be underdressed in blue jeans. However, there's a noticeable difference between the manner of dress for men and women, with women generally wearing high-heeled shoes (always and everywhere), lots of jewellery and dressy clothing. Men, on the other hand, most often wear slacks, long-sleeved shirts or sweaters and black leather shoes.

Cultural Tolerance

One of the most wonderful things about Syrians is that they are quite open toward and accepting of the differences between themselves and Westerners. Any behaviour or manner of dress that is unusual to them will be the topic of humourous or puzzled discussion. But the talk won't be malicious, nor are you likely to be rejected for your behaviour as long as it's in good faith. They seem to be in tune with your intentions.

Welcome to My Building

A young student told me of her welcoming visit to an American couple who had recently moved into her building. A large bouquet of flowers in hand, she knocked on their door. The man came to the door and said, "Yes?" and my student proceeded in her limited English to welcome them to Syria. He took the flowers with a "Thank you" and put them in a vase while she stood in the open doorway. At about the same time, the man's wife came into the living room and greeted my student briefly, then said, "Thanks for the flowers. We have to go now." With this, they both headed out the door, past the young Syrian, without finding out who she was, offering to have her back when they would be home or any other civility. The young woman bore no apparent hostility toward the people but was baffled by their behaviour. I assured her that such behaviour was not typical of all Americans, especially those who live abroad.

Syrian hospitality can be overwhelming at times: some people practically 'adopt' you, showering you with gifts and invitations. Even Syrians who criticise the foreign policies of Western governments graciously accept citizens of such countries—especially Americans—as part of their own family. They recognise people as separate from their governments— something a lot of Americans could do a much better job of. I have been invited to stop and have tea with a peasant family while walking through a village, struggling to communicate in my limited Damascene Arabic; Bedouin children have invited me to their tents or tiny huts for tea when they saw me hiking in the desert; as I was walking through an oasis in the desert, an old man on a bicycle stopped and without saying a word handed me pieces of candy, then rode on; and people I barely know in Damascus have given me a standing invitation to visit their homes at any time.

SOME PRECAUTIONS

Because Syrians are so accepting, and because they are in tune with your intentions, there are few taboos. But respecting their cultural sensitivities will endear you to them and help fight negative stereotypes about Westerners.

Manner of Dress

Although Syria has no official dress code, most people, Christian or Muslim, dress (sexually) modestly. In particular they do not expose much flesh. You may wear shorts and T-shirts walking around the streets of Damascus, Aleppo or ancient ruins (although you will draw attention to yourself); but when you go to a Syrian's home or out with a Syrian group, it is wise to dress modestly: no shorts, no sleeveless or strapless tops, exposed bellies, etc. It's unlikely your hosts will react negatively to you, but it may offend them.

Alcohol

Nearly every kind of alcoholic beverage is available in Syria, although only a few shops and restaurants sell it. In fact, some of the local beers are quite delicious and unbelievably inexpensive—try Damascus' own Barada beer. Most Christians and even some Muslims drink a little, but drunkenness is rare—in fact, people found drunk in public are often jailed overnight. If you go to a Muslim home, the hosts are not likely to offer you an alcoholic drink, and they will often apologise for not being able to do so. If you go to a restaurant with Muslims and the restaurant serves alcohol, they might let you know they won't mind if you order a drink; a few will even have one themselves. But if you imbibe, moderation is required. If you get drunk, you will offend your hosts.

Sexual Jokes, etc.

In a group of men only, or of women only, sex is a favourite topic, and moderately dirty jokes are enjoyed, especially by men. But avoid making such jokes or even discussing sexual topics in mixed company. It is likely to embarrass and offend everyone. Likewise, terribly explicit sexual jokes or toilet humour may be offensive, even in an all-male group.

Footwear

Shoes bear a special significance in the Arab world. To begin with, they must be removed before entering a mosque. This practice stems from the story of God telling Moses at the burning bush to remove his shoes because he was standing on holy ground.

The custom extends to most traditional homes as well, and street shoes are removed as soon as anyone enters. The family wears 'house shoes'—slippers or sandals—that never touch the ground outside. In older houses there are even sandals used only for the toilet. The reason is that the squat toilet in older homes, a ceramic toilet bowl set into the floor, has no cistern to flush it. It is 'flushed' by using a small hose, and the flushing keeps the floor in the small room wet. Thus the need for 'toilet shoes'. New homes have regular flushing tanks—although the toilets may still be the squatting kind—and most even have bidets.

Since shoe soles carry such significance for uncleanness, they also carry some social taboos. One is that you never put your feet on a footstool, coffee table or desk when an Arab is in the room with you. Showing the bottoms of your shoes will cause social discomfort because it's quite insulting in Arab culture. Likewise, do not cross your legs with one ankle or calf on the other leg, because this also exposes one sole. To put your shoes on furniture (lying on a couch or bed with your shoes on, for example) is, of course, also not acceptable.

It is humiliating and an insult to hit an Arab with the bottom of a shoe. A friend in Syria told me a story about a Syrian woman who, weary of being harassed by men on the streets, began carrying an old shoe in her purse. Whenever a man grabbed or touched her or made lewd noises or comments to her, she smacked him on the head or shoulder with the shoe, thus publicly humiliating him.

BEHAVIOUR BETWEEN WOMEN AND MEN

A foreign man who is accustomed to touching female friends at home must be cautious here. Despite the fact that Middle Eastern and Mediterranean men (a minority, certainly, but a sizable minority) are infamous for their crudity toward foreign women, often grabbing women's buttocks, breasts or crotches whenever they think they can get away with it, it is absolutely unacceptable for a foreign man to touch an Arab woman, regardless of how innocent the intent. Don't even expect to shake a woman's hand unless she makes the first move (which, by the way, is common among younger, educated women). The odd thing about this is that in crowded public spaces, you can come into nearly full-body contact with the opposite gender, and it isn't even acknowledged; women often brushed up against me as if I weren't there; in fact, one time in a post office, I was nearly knocked over by an older woman who banged full into me with her breasts! I was quite shocked and didn't know how to react, but she acted as if I weren't even there. The only touching that seems to be taboo is with the hands.

While touching seems to be the only restriction on men, vis-à-vis Arab women, Western women must behave formally with Arab men. I, for example, can be verbally friendly to a Syrian woman, and there is no implication that I'm trying to 'get close' to her. But a Western woman who is at all friendly or even makes eye contact with men on the street will make those men think she 'desires' them. It takes no encouragement whatsoever for an Arab man to make passes at a Western woman; and if she responds in any manner that's perceived as accepting, the man automatically thinks he has a 'chance' with her. This is a sad and sorry situation but is as old as civilisation here and one must learn to cope with it.

SETTLING IN

'... wherever he laid his hat was his home ...'
—*Papa Was A Rolling Stone* by The Temptations

LIVING IN SYRIA CAN BE UNCERTAIN and trying at first. Even if you have a car and speak Arabic fairly well, you cannot help but notice the amount of time and effort day-to-day living requires. Shopping for things you want is like hunting and gathering, and dealing with the bureaucracy can baffle and frustrate a newcomer. Just about anything you could accomplish quickly and efficiently at home (in Western countries, at any rate) usually takes much longer in Syria and presents one obstacle after another. After a while, you learn where to find most of your shopping needs and how to take shortcuts. The information in this chapter is predominantly for Damascus, since that is where most of Syria's foreign residents live.

There's a lot of the 'rolling stone' in expatriates. And one nice thing about Syria—Damascus in particular, since that's where more than 90 per cent of the foreign residents live—is the variety of places to lay your hat. If you're a single person kicking around the Middle East, maybe studying Arabic, you can live on the cheap by finding a room with a Syrian family (most commonly in the old city) for as little as the equivalent of US$ 100 per month. On the other hand, if you have a sizable family and want to live like aristocrats, replete with live-in servants, you can do so cheaper than in any Western country, although that seems to be changing rapidly.

Despite the fact that most young people in the cities have to live with their parents until well into their twenties or thirties, there is no shortage of rental units for foreigners. In fact, this is one reason young people often cannot leave home: landlords can rent a decent apartment to someone from Germany, the United States or Japan for many times what they could to a Syrian. Also, rent controls make it nearly impossible for a landlord to evict someone, foreign or native.

Expats from Western countries, however, usually find rents that, although outrageous by Syrian standards, are much lower than what they might pay at home for a similar unit, so they tend not to bargain very hard. They are also here for a limited time, after which the landlord can increase the rent. For these reasons, landlords and the house rental agents who serve them often refuse to rent to Syrians, preferring instead the wealthier and less troublesome temporary foreign residents.

FINDING A HOME

Unless you work for an embassy or a company that makes housing arrangements for you, you will need to deal with a house agent. They are ubiquitous in areas where foreigners live, but before you contact one, ask your embassy, company or other trusted expats for recommendations; the honesty of many agents is questionable, just as it might be in the West. It would be particularly wise to avoid those with elaborate offices or those who drive new luxury cars. I had dealings with several agents and the most trustworthy ones I found didn't even have cars—they showed apartments by taxi.

Location

Some foreigners prefer to move into old neighbourhoods with an authentic traditional atmosphere. If you do this, you may find less apartment selection, fewer amenities, and more noise, but you will also save considerably on your rent and experience more cultural immersion.

If you want more of the comforts of home, a larger and more elaborate apartment, and more contact with the international community, the main neighbourhoods to consider in Damascus are Abu Romaneh, Rawda, Malki,

Mouhajerine and Mezzeh (a suburb on the southwest edge of town). These are where you will find most embassies and UN offices, most foreigners and the widest variety of goods for sale. Apartments in these areas range from traditionally Syrian to elaborately modern and palatial.

If you live on or near a busy street, the noise will keep you awake if your bedroom windows face the street. Vehicles without mufflers, blaring horns, loud voices, the air horns used by heating oil salesmen and propane peddlers banging on metal containers are unavoidable anywhere in the city but are louder and more relentless on busy streets. If you must have peace and quiet, your only options in Damascus are Mezzeh (if your house is off the highway) and Dummar—a housing project to the northwest that is sometimes just called 'the project'. But these are not viable options unless you have a car and don't mind spending a lot of time commuting.

Home heating oil delivered by a horsedrawn tanker in an old quarter of Damascus.

Another thing to consider about location is that you are more likely to get burglarised if you live in an area full of expats than if you live on a less-travelled street in a neighbourhood with few foreigners and a stable Syrian population.

Price and Amenities

Damascus has higher rents than other cities in Syria, although they are generally lower than in North American or European capitals (a fact that seems to be changing rapidly). Along with tourism, the increase in oil exploration and production, the vast number of refugees from Iraq, and increasing wealth has come a steady rise in rents. During 1991–93, rental charges increased around 25 per cent annually. This was not so much due to a housing shortage but rather to a get-what-the-market-will-bear mentality that had developed among house agents and landlords.

Dishonest Housing Agents

A Mauritanian man I knew who worked for a housing agent in Damascus railed about the dishonesty of many Syrian agents: "Most agents jack up the rent asked by the landlord and split the increase with the landlord. They know they can ask just about any amount and the embassies will pay the price." Landowners and house agents have some of the highest incomes in Syria. A recently renovated, two-bedroom, top-floor apartment I rented for 30,000 SP (US$ 600) per month—because I refused to pay more—was rented before me by a Japanese man for 50,000 SP (US$ 1,000) per month. To him the rent was low by Tokyo standards, while to me 50,000 SP was too high.

If you want a basic apartment and are willing to live in older areas of the city, you can still find small, decent apartments for less than US$ 500 per month at this time, but that may change soon. If you are willing to live in a room in a centuries-old house in the old city, you may get by for less than US$ 100 however, and may be able to share some of your host family's meals.

At the other extreme, a large, newly renovated apartment with lots of amenities in a desirable area (particularly Abu Romaneh and Mezzeh) can cost you well over US$ 2,000 per month. According to my Syrian friend, housing prices have gone up quite dramatically since the turn of the millennium—in some cases by as much as 50–60 per cent, and real estate agents say they've increased around 40 per cent in only the past two years, so you should be prepared to bargain hard. This dramatic increase is perhaps not so much because of the whatever-the-market-will-bear mentality, though; according to recent reports from the US Associated Press, the UN Refugee Agency and other sources, more than half of the two million plus Iraqi refugees fleeing civil war, crime and the invasion forces in their homeland are in Syria—with the largest number in Damascus. In fact, the UN Refugee Agency states that those refugees make up nearly 5 per cent of Syria's population! According to reports from Damascus, some whole neighbourhoods—for example, the Jarramana suburb of Damascus and the al Yarmouk Palestinian refugee camp—which itself has become a sprawling suburb of the capital—have become dominated by Iraqi refugees so that only Iraqi Arabic (a dialect quite different from that of Damascus) can be heard in some areas. Also, around 150,000 Lebanese fled into Syria when Israel invaded that country in 2006. There are complaints among much of the affected Syrian population that all these refugees have driven the price of real estate up by as much as 300 per cent in the past few years. It seems dubious to me that refugees who had to flee their homeland with little more than the clothes on their back and the cash in their pockets could be responsible for any dramatic increase in housing prices, but the sheer numbers have no doubt had some effect.

Most two- or three-bedroom units have a full bath and another room with an Arab toilet (a toilet bowl set into the floor) and a sink and mirror outside the toilet room. The biggest, most expensive units often have servants' quarters.

Before renting an apartment, there are many things to look over and negotiate. Landlords are usually willing to make a lot of commitments in order to get you on a year's lease; but once you've signed and paid, their attitudes can change dramatically. (And don't forget that it's common to require three to six months' rent in advance, so be

prepared to dish out a big chunk of cash up front.) Here are some things to look for.

Paint and Water Leaks

Top-floor apartments, unless they have sloped roofs, are notorious for leaking during winter rains. Leaks are easy to spot on ceilings and upper walls, and if you move in after the rains start, the problem cannot be fixed until the following summer.

Conversely, lower-floor apartments have problems with moisture in the walls that erodes the masonry and paint so badly that a freshly painted wall can look diseased within a few months. If you see signs of serious bubbling, blistering, or peeling—even under a fresh coat of paint—insist on having the problem repaired at its source before moving in. My first bottom floor apartment had such a severe moisture problem in one wall that paint wouldn't stick and the plaster fell off. The owner did not want to tear out the wall to get to the root of the problem, so I moved out.

Plumbing

Most plumbing systems here are antiquated and probably did not work well to begin with. One serious problem in ground-floor apartments is sewer backups; another is foul odours, especially during cold weather when the house is closed up. Also, water pressure may be weak. My top-floor apartment had so little pressure that the shower couldn't be used. This happens sometimes when the water storage tank is only a few metres above the shower head. Also, some drains don't work well. Most tend to plug up easily (in some older buildings you can't throw tissue into the toilet bowls), and if you pull the plug quickly from a full bathtub or a sink full of soapy dishwater, the water may back up through the floor drain.

All apartments should also have a kitchen faucet that brings in fresh water from outside for drinking. Except for water from rooftop tanks (the tanks may not be clean), tap water in Damascus is drinkable, fresh and sweet. It comes from springs in the mountains and is lightly treated with chlorine. Make sure the apartment has an operating water storage tank for those times in late summer and autumn when there are water cuts. If you have water stored, you can shower, cook and wash clothes if the main pipeline is turned off; without it, you'll suffer during the hottest time of the year.

Electrical

Regular blackouts in many areas outside the capital make special electrical equipment desirable. For many years, electricity was off everywhere in Syria for several hours a day. Although this problem seems to have been fixed in Damascus, the rest of the country still suffers blackouts at least occasionally.

Before renting an apartment, it's best to check with a reliable source to determine if your location has uninterrupted electrical service. If it does not, you should insist on one of two systems to reduce this inconvenience. The cheapest one is a battery system that gives you some lights and outlets for fans, radios, stereos, televisions and small appliances while the main current is off. When the electricity is restored the batteries automatically recharge and the only maintenance required is adding distilled water to the cells every few months. The system is easy to install and you will be glad to have it, especially for a fan

Stabilisers

in the summer and lights on dreary winter days. You cannot use hairdryers, refrigerators, air conditioners or washing machines on these batteries.

The more expensive option is a gasoline- or diesel-powered generator. Some newer upscale buildings have these for all units, but they can be added to almost any apartment. The advantage over the battery system is that all outlets, lights and appliances (except A/C) work with the generator.

Even when the electricity is on, the voltage sometimes fluctuates dramatically—particularly in the evening for several hours after darkness falls and in the hottest parts of summer when most people are using A/C units; it often gets so low that a washing machine won't spin and your heating system won't work if the stove or boiler has electronic ignition. This seems to be worse on upper floors because the lower floors use up most of the buildings' voltage. (One theory is that in older buildings the power lines come in at the bottom and floors are hooked to it successively, so when lower floors are using a lot of power and the incoming voltage is low anyway, the line is drained before it gets to the top floors.) An easy and simple solution is a voltage stabiliser.

Syria's voltage is 220, so you might also ask the landlord or house agent to provide you with a 220-volt to 110-volt transformer if you're coming from North America. These are inexpensive but are heavy and bulky, so you won't take it with you when you leave. The small plug-in type transformers you can buy in the United States and Canada are likely to burn out if you use them for kitchen appliances or hairdryers.

Finally, look for safety hazards in the wiring. It seems there are either no electrical building codes or no enforcement of codes, and wires often hang loose everywhere. It is also not uncommon for outlets, lights and light switches to be in a shower or tub area where one wrong move could electrocute someone.

Furnishings and Kitchen Utensils

All apartments are furnished, but there are often big differences in the quality and quantity of provisions. Some of the furniture is dirty and uncomfortable. Again, if you want something changed, make sure it's done before you pay a deposit. Most landlords and rental agents I encountered offered everything from new kitchen cabinets to new furniture of my choice. Take advantage of this desire to have you as a tenant—especially if the rent asked for is high and you can't negotiate them downwards.

Telephone

Most apartments have telephones, although some are shared with other parties. If a telephone, particularly a private line, is important to you, don't take the landlord's word that he/ she can get one for you if there isn't already one in the unit. Also, make sure it's in and operating before you take the apartment; it still may take years to get a phone line. On the other hand, some sources say there are more than 8 million cell phone users in Syria, and the price of the cell phone and service is not notably higher than it is in Western countries, so a land line in your house may be of moot value. I highly recommend getting a cell phone, and many Westerners use theirs to keep in contact with home, thus avoiding the regular hassles involved with long-distance calls from land-based lines.

Heating System

Examine the heating systems. Older and smaller apartments often have heating oil (called *mazott*) stoves (*sobia*) that make you cosy and comfortable when you're near them, but cold if you aren't. In small apartments this is no problem, but a single *sobia* will not warm a large apartment well. The stoves are generally Syrian-made, inexpensive and work fairly well, so insist on another if you think there's a chance you'll need it: winters in Syria can be quite cold. Some newer *sobias* have electrical ignition (a good reason to have a voltage stabiliser) and fans. These keep several rooms toasty warm, but more distant ones are cold.

A more common type of heating in new and refurbished buildings is hot water central heating. This also uses *mazott* to heat the water, is ignited electrically and keeps the house an even temperature throughout. For either kind of heat, find out where your *mazott* storage tank is and how full it is when you move in. Don't accept having to buy your heating oil a little at a time from a neighbour or landlord as they may not be around when you run out. In a large apartment, 500 litres will last a couple of months when the weather is moderate. The problem is that it may take several days to get the oil if it's an especially cold winter. There is also sometimes a *mazott* shortage in January and February.

If your apartment is not blasted by direct summer sunlight and is not on the top floor of a building, you can probably get by without air-conditioning, but it is nice, especially if you have trouble sleeping when it's hot. In late summer and early autumn, it does not cool down a lot at nights. If you live on a top floor and/or have large windows that face the afternoon and evening sun, I recommend air-conditioning—Syrian summers get very hot. The last August I lived there, the daytime temperatures were over 40°C (104°F) for several weeks, and the nights cooled down only to the lower 30s. The air is intensely dry, however, so even a large fan can cool you during the middle of the night. Basically, what you need for cooling depends on your body's tolerance for extreme, dry heat.

Time of Power Outages

Regular, daily blackouts seem to be a thing of the past now, at least in Damascus. But the situation could change for the worse again. Find out if your apartment will be without electricity regularly, and if so, find out the usual times. In the past, the most common times were from 7–8 am until 10 am–noon and from 1–2 pm to 4–6 pm, although in

neighbourhoods where few foreigners or wealthy Syrians live, it may be longer. In all neighbourhoods it is common for the time to change unannounced.

Windows and Screens

Mosquitoes are a terrible nuisance from late summer until the first cold period, usually in late November or early December. For this reason, make sure that at least some windows have screens (without holes) or you'll be devoured when you most need to keep your windows open. Even with screens, you may have mosquitoes, but an electric repellent that is available there will keep them away while you sleep.

If your apartment is on or near the ground, make sure all windows lock. If they're especially easy to reach, ask for protective bars—they could save you from a burglary; although rare, they do happen. My top floor apartment was burglarised while I was away for several days, and I lost a couple thousand US dollars cash, a couple of expensive watches and some irreplaceable jewellery. Even one of the cabinet ministers in the mid-90s suffered an attempted burglary while he had a large chunk of cash in his house.

Satellite TV

Although Syria doesn't yet have cable TV, it does have satellite systems. The dishes cost around US$ 100–200 as of 2005, and you may be able to negotiatefor your rental agent or landlord to purchase one for you if your apartment doesn't already have one. After you get the dish, you pay a fairly low monthly charge for numerous channels. Without a dish, your choices for TV are pretty severely limited.

THE CONTRACT AND PAYMENT

Most landlords want a one-year contract, but the standard contract states that if your government requires you to leave the country before its completion, you are entitled to a pro-rated refund. But what if your landlord says he/she does not have the money for a refund? The norm at this time is to sign a one-year contract but to pay for only three or six months at a time. This gives you leverage on the landlord for needed repairs, which there will be. Broken or exploding water heaters, water storage tanks with split seams, clogged drains, water leaks, broken appliances and smoking stoves are all common.

Insist on a contract signed by the landlord before you pay; never make a handshake agreement. Also, investigate the agreed-upon repairs and improvements and make sure they are completed to your satisfaction before you pay. A Canadian woman who lived in Damascus paid a deposit of several hundred dollars for the landlord to buy some promised furniture for an apartment; when she moved in, the furniture had not been purchased and she was unable to get her deposit back.

Immediately after you move in, it's wise to have your outer door locks changed and not give your landlord or house agent a key.

Some landlords want tenants to pay hard currency. This is unwise because it still may mean two trips out of the country for each payment: one to deposit your cheque and another, two to three weeks later, to get the cash. (At this time—although the situation may change with new banking regulations and competition—you cannot exchange

Syrian pounds (SP) for hard currency within the country.)
Also, if you take advantage of unofficial exchange rates
during the winter when they are highest, you can benefit
by paying in pounds. Whatever your mode of payment,
get a receipt (in English, if you don't read Arabic) with all
the pertinent information.

UTILITY CHARGES

Electricity bills come regularly about every two months. If
your usage is light, the average payment should be around
1,000–2,000 SP (US$ 20–40) per month for a family with a
two- or three-bedroom apartment, 500–800 SP (US$ 10–16)
per month for a single person with a small apartment and
no airconditioning. Heavy airconditioning use can drive the
cost higher, of course.

Landlords generally pay the water bills because they're so
low: about 20–30 SP monthly.

Telephone bills generally come several months after the
calls are made, which creates a serious problem for Syrians
who rent to foreigners. It is common for them to require
either a letter of guaranty from your employer or embassy
or a deposit of several thousand pounds before allowing you
international phone service. If you can do neither of these,
you may be able to use your telephone for local calls only.
International calls are expensive, running around 125 SP per
minute, and the rate climbs after the first 20 minutes. Lower
rates are in effect from 2 am to 7 am.

Making International Calls

From most telephones you can dial your own international
calls, but if you have trouble getting through, the international
operators (143 or 144) will help you. Most of them speak limited
English and/or French.

Ovens and stoves operate almost exclusively from bottled
propane (called *ghaaz*), which at this time costs around
200 SP each. The *ghaaz* sellers cruise the streets in their
micro pickups, banging on the cans and calling out, "*Ghaaz,*

ghaaz! Ghaaz, ghaaz!" For a single person who does little cooking at home, a bottle may last a year; for a family who does a lot of cooking, perhaps only a month. At any rate, it's a bargain. Some newer stoves have an electric burner and broiler as well. This is beneficial if your gas runs out just as you're starting to prepare breakfast or have guests coming for dinner and cannot find a gas peddler. Oven temperatures are not easy to regulate and seem uneven from one unit to another.

The price of heating oil is regulated by the government, and it increased the price in 2002 at the same time that it raised most government workers' salaries by 20 per cent. The new price is about 8.45 SP (roughly US$ 0.16) per litre. Get a recommendation from someone you trust before filling your tank; if you don't, you may be charged for more than you get or end up with watered-down *mazott* that won't burn well.

Appliances You Won't Find

Clothes dryers, microwaves, automatic dishwashers and garbage disposals are still rare in Syria. Those that exist are generally imported by embassies and a few wealthy Syrians for their own use. You hang your clothes up to dry, heat your food conventionally and take your trash to the nearest dumpster, which may be as far as two blocks away.

THINGS TO BRING WITH YOU

Apartments in the cities are pretty well outfitted, and you can negotiate for things you need. There are some things, though, that are either not available or very expensive and not likely to be provided by the landlord.

Kitchens

You can buy most small kitchen appliances here except French coffee presses, percolators, coffee bean and spice grinders, and waffle irons; the drawback is that any imported items are very expensive. If you use such things, it's best to bring them with you.

Handmade glass bowls, glasses and cups are a Syrian specialty and unbelievably cheap. You can have the glass blowers make anything you want for next to nothing. Also, landlords are expected to furnish completely functional kitchens. You may not care for the styles provided, but kitchen equipment is heavy and difficult to pack; it may be cheaper and easier to buy dishes, pots and pans there if you can't persuade your landlord to provide them.

Towels and Linens

Beds vary in size from singles and cot-styles to king-size. Some have sets of springs under a mattress, some are futon-style mattresses over boards and others are just a foam pad on a board. If soft pillows are essential for your comfort, bring your own. Your own sheets from home may not fit your bed in Syria, and you can have a set of sheets made for half what they would cost in North America or Europe. Specify that they should be fitted sheets—giving clear instructions—if that is your preference.

Don't expect to find conveniences like bath washcloths. I haven't seen one anywhere from eastern Syria to Greece, or from Turkey to Jordan and Egypt. Towels are easy to find, however, and if they aren't thick and absorbent, at least they dry quickly.

DOMESTIC HELP

You can hire nannies, housekeepers, live-in servants and houseboys inexpensively. There are many Indians, Pakistanis, Sri Lankans and Filipinas/os who are here for those jobs, and they are generally dependable, honest and do a decent job. You can hire a Syrian woman as a maid, cook or housekeeper for approximately half of what you'd pay a foreigner, but she will only speak Arabic. Having domestic help is a status symbol few diplomats and wealthy Syrians do without.

There is no shortage of domestic help in Syria. One can simply check with other expats or wealthier Syrians to find several people looking for domestic work. Some will only clean, others will cook and clean and iron, and yet others will take care of children; some will live in, while others will work only a set number of hours. Most diplomatic personnel and wealthy Syrians have live-in or full-time help, while the less wealthy may simply have someone come to clean and iron once or twice a week. You shouldn't have to pay more than a few hundred SP per hour for Indians, Filipinas, Sri Lankans, or Pakistanis who come to clean periodically, and Syrians generally charge even less.

While most of the domestics are honest (any foreigner who gets caught stealing would be deported immediately), there are some things to be careful of. One is that the foreign help may use your telephone to call their families in their home country without your permission or knowledge. One family I knew discovered US$ 600 worth of phone calls to Sri Lanka. Another common problem is petty theft that can add up to something substantial over time. While it's highly unlikely that any domestic help would steal such things as computers, VCRs or televisions, some may take small things or small amounts of cash now and then, thinking you'll never notice.

Another problem that's unrelated to honesty is a lacka-daisical attitude about time and commitments. Your domestic may promise to come at 12 noon every Wednesday, for example, but rarely come on time or, worse yet, not come regularly and not call to let you know he/she won't be there and why. This seems to be true of all domestics there, whatever their nationality.

Domestic help should not be paid in advance, although some will try to get you to do so. Those who come periodically are generally paid after each session, while those who live in or work full-time are usually paid either once or twice per month—normally around US$ 200–300 per month. Full-time and live-in help normally have only one day off each week and two weeks to a month of vacation each year. The vacation varies a great deal, depending on the nationality of the employers and what they are accustomed to. There seems to be no custom of bonuses for domestic help, but small gifts or cash for birthdays, Christmas (for Christian domestics) or Eid (for Muslims) are greatly appreciated. Domestic helpers also appreciate donations of used clothing or household items you no longer want. Even if they can't use the items or don't want them for themselves, they always seem to know others who are in need of them.

If you have a full-time or live-in servant, that person should be responsible to supervise any part-time or occasional domestic help you have. The former also commonly do grocery shopping and run all kinds of errands, and most domestic help can baby sit children for a night out or pets for several days or weeks if you're away.

Hiring domestic help is painless: it's most often done informally, with no paperwork or government reports. Firing foreign workers is also quite easy since domestics are not covered by the country's employment laws that make it so difficult to fire regular Syrian employees.

URBAN TRANSPORTATION

Despite extensive public transportation, getting around can be tedious and time-consuming, although that seems to be less so now than a couple of decades ago and will likely be

Airport Transfers

A company called Transtour, which uses a fleet of Volvos, will pick you up promptly at any hour for a ride to the airport and charges about the same fare as regular taxis. For dependable pickup service, call the Transtour office in the Sheraton Hotel and schedule the time and place.

even better in the future with the new transportation systems that are being introduced.

Taxis

Public transportation in Syria is very cheap. You can go nearly anywhere in Damascus or Aleppo for less than 50 Syrian pounds (SP), and a ride in the central part of a city rarely costs more than 20-30 SP, including a tip.

But there are drawbacks to using taxis. Simply getting one during rush hour is often difficult—as it is in any major city anywhere in the world. They are also small and uncomfortable for tall or large people (all seem to be Japanese or Korean mini-cars). Make sure the driver resets his meter when he picks you up. If he refuses, get out and catch another one—he probably intends to overcharge you. In fact don't be surprised if when you get to your destination the fare your driver charges is more than what is on the meter. If this happens, simply give him the fare on the meter plus a reasonable tip. Carrying small change will help you to avoid being overcharged in this manner.

Buses

At this time, there are two types of in-city buses: government-operated buses and privately run mini vans.

A ride in government-operated buses costs only a few pounds per person. It's an interesting experience to ride these, as you'll see a big variety of people on them. There are several drawbacks though. Buses are usually packed during rush hour, with people hanging out of the doors, and even though smoking is banned, the rule is ignored. Another is that schedules are not published, and those posted on each bus are seldom reliable. Unless you are quite proficient at reading Arabic, you can't tell where the bus is headed: bus numbers and destinations are only in Arabic.

The ubiquitous new mini vans are privately owned and the standard fare is now only a few pounds for most in-city rides. They are stricter about the no-smoking rule, won't accept riders they don't have seats for and are more dependable time-wise. Mini buses will also stop almost anywhere along their routes to pick you up or drop you off, much as a taxi would. They also travel between cities and the surrounding villages. The biggest drawback again is that numbers and destinations are printed only in Arabic, although it's easier to ask the driver where he's headed than it is on the big transports.

Giving directions to a taxi driver and understanding the destination of a bus can be difficult because there are no addresses, only neighbourhoods and landmarks, and sometimes building names. Besides, many streets are known by their old names (pre-1970), not by the names you see on city maps.

Your Own Vehicle

If your employer provides your transportation, consider yourself fortunate. Cars bought in Syria are prohibitively priced for most people due to tariffs of up to 150 per cent (down from the 256 per cent of the early 90s). Also, the supply is limited, although increasing as new importers set up business. These things make even old cars expensive: a 1983 Colt or other small Japanese model, in good shape, may cost double what the car cost new. Kept long enough, automobiles have become a genuine investment here, always increasing in value. However, after the tariff was reduced, all cars immediately lost about half their previous value, enraging Syrians who had just recently bought cars.

There are several things to consider before buying a vehicle. One is that parking in the cities, particularly Damascus, is a major problem. There are no parking garages and little on-street parking. Also, it is nerve wracking to drive in the chaotic Arab city traffic—and you can be certain that your car will at least get scratched or dented. If you are unlucky enough to have an accident, it often takes weeks or even months for repairs.

On the other hand, if you live in the central city, you can get around most of the time on foot.

The good news for those aspiring to drive their own cars is that auto insurance is not expensive by American or European standards; and you can probably recoup most of the price of the vehicle when you sell it.

There are several ways to go about buying a car. If you want a new one, there is a duty-free auto sales area at Adra where the government sells new vehicles without the usual tariffs. You must be sponsored by your employer in order to buy here, and your employer will be a co-owner of the vehicle. The bureaucratic process requires letters from your employer to the Ministry of Culture and the Ministry of Foreign Affairs. Once you get the vehicle, you take it to the Ministry of Transportation (at the east end of Baghdad Street) to register, pay fees and get a license.

The process for a used car is less tedious, but perhaps riskier. You find a local party who wants to sell one, negotiate a price, then have the party go through all the necessary procedures with you, including paying the taxes and legitimately transferring ownership. Currently, you can buy a junker (a 1970 American land yacht, for example) for around 100,000 SP (about US$ 2,000, including taxes). Newer, more dependable cars may cost more than 500,000 SP.

Auto Parts, Accessories, Repairs

Immediately east and southeast of the Karnak bus station in the Baramkeh area of Damascus is an auto souk that includes tyre shops and repair shops. Other repair shops are scattered throughout the perimeter of Damascus and on the outskirts of all cities and larger villages. These mechanics are masters at keeping the 30-, 40-, 50-, and even 60-year-old vehicles that populate the streets and highways of Syria running and so no doubt have excellent skills.

Bicycles

For the brave souls willing to risk life and limb on the streets of cities, bicycles are an option. You won't yet find many high-tech Japanese, American or French brands, though; the majority are heavy old Chinese-made clunkers with one speed and one colour: black. You can occasionally find a Chinese-made ten-speed or three-speed, but they are also quite heavy. The price is attractive, however: a used one may only cost around 2,000 SP. A bicycle souk near Al Maghribeeyeh Circle sells bikes, parts and accessories and does repairs. There is also a difficult-to-find bicycle souk in the old city.

Fridays, especially in the morning and during the afternoon siesta, are good days to cycle in the city because traffic is light.

DEALING WITH BUREAUCRACY

Syria's history as a nation has been dominated by socialism, which has created a massive bureaucracy and all the rules and procedures necessary to feed the monster. No task is simple when dealing with the government: you go to one desk, pay your fee of a few Syrian pounds and pick up an application; then you buy several stamps (all government documents require stamps); make photocopies of your passport and letter from your employer; take your completed application to a different office for a signature; take the assortment of papers back to a different desk; and so on...

Government office hours are generally from 8:30 or 9 am to 1:30 or 2 pm, Saturday through Thursday. Few clerks in these offices speak anything but Arabic, although they usually understand a few English, French or German words. If you have something critical to attend to and your Arabic is not strong, it's best to take an interpreter with you.

Iqaamas

If you work here, even for a few months, it's advisable to get a residence visa (*iqaama*). The main advantage is that it gives you the same in-country hotel rates that Syrian nationals get, which is about a quarter the tourist rate. This means you can go to Palmyra, for example, and stay at the lovely Zenobia Hotel, on the edge of the ruins, for 500 SP (US$ 10) per night!

The first step for an *iqaama* is to get an AIDS test at a government health office. In Damascus this is in a neighbourhood known as Zeblatanee, about halfway between

A stay at the lovely Hotel Wadi beneath Krak de Chevalier on the hill costs very little if you have an *iqaama*.

Abbaseeyin Circle and Baab Touma. You pay in the basement, go to the second floor for the test, then return two days later (after noon) for the results. Take the certificate to the passport and immigration office, pay for an application, go through the usual stamps and signature routines, then wait for several months. The AIDS test now costs 500 SP (US$ 10) per person, and every member of your family must have one except babies. Until you get your *iqaama*, you will have a receipt for your application stapled in your passport. Unfortunately, however, this receipt will not give you the resident hotel discounts, and you also may have trouble getting an exit/return visa to travel out of the country before you get your *iqaama*.

Post Office

The Syrian postal service is notoriously unreliable and censored as well, although recent attempts to emphasise service may slowly change some of that. While living there, I sent several letters and manuscripts out of the country that never made it to their destination. Also, two boxes of gifts mailed from the United States never arrived and two letters, also from the United States, vanished.

The advantage of using the Syrian post office for international mail is the cost: a letter to another Arab country costs less than US$ 0.20 and a letter to Europe costs only about double that. For any critical mail, however, use your country's diplomatic pouch service or a courier service. The latter is reliable and fast (72 hours), but quite expensive by Syrian standards—at least 800 SP (US$ 16).

If you wish to send anything other than regular mail through the Syrian postal system, you must take the empty box and its contents (including the stuffing and wrapping) to the central post office and allow customs officials to inspect it. They will then watch you pack and seal it for shipping and put a tag on it. Then you take it to a special window for mailing. Do not ship anything irreplaceable this way; use a courier service or shipping company.

For incoming packages, you go to the same post office and open the carton for official inspection. Check with your local post office before coming to Syria for a list of restricted or forbidden in-bound items. There is no door-to-door mail delivery in Syria: to get mail you need your own PO box or the use of your employer's, your embassy's or a friend's.

The Police

Whenever you move into new living quarters you must immediately register with the police. It is best to have your house agent or landlord assist you with this, so you register at the appropriate police station. The cost is minimal. If they do not offer you a yellow card with their stamp on it, request one—it's your proof that you have registered.

Pedestrians can cross the street anywhere, even against red lights, and the police ignore them (although in the early 1990s, there was a crackdown on jay-walkers, and some folks actually spent a night in jail for it). Unless you drive you won't have any dealings with the traffic police. If you do drive, their presence at most major intersections is intended to maintain order. Pay attention to their traffic directing attempts. Few streets or highways in Syria have posted speed limits, and those that exist are totally ignored. About the only way you'll get stopped for speeding is if you're caught going outrageously fast. It seemed that no matter how fast I drove on the highways, most other traffic outpaced me.

The laws in Syria, however, favour those not driving, and the driver who hits a poor man's donkey and kills it or injures a pedestrian or cyclist is considered at fault and must pay damages. In the event that you are accused of a crime or are victimised by a burglar, rapist or thief, you will have to deal with the crime police. It's best to contact your embassy's security section first and let them make the initial contact with the police. Each branch of the police has its own special functions. For example, the homicide branch actually investigates all violent crimes and major thefts. Except for a pistol tucked into their belt, these police officers are indistinguishable from other men on the street; they wear no uniforms or other visible identification. Police procedures are obscure and baffling, all the more so if your Arabic is limited.

As a rule, non-Arab foreigners in Syria are allowed quite a bit of leeway by the police, whether they're driving or involved in any other daily activity. The two things most likely to get a visitor in trouble are drug-related activities and harsh criticism of or activity against the government. Possession of or dealing in drugs will definitely land you in jail, and activity against the government will get you deported. Religious proselytising is also illegal, although I know of no one who's been arrested for this activity.

The Secret Police (Mukhabarat)

This is a massive organisation whose mere mention makes most Syrians uncomfortable. No one is sure who works for the organisation or is an informer. The Mukhabarat has numerous branches, two of which deal primarily with foreigners. They investigate non-Syrians who apply for visas and *iqaamas*, and some teachers at the American Language Centre assume there are informers in most classes. However, there were only two cases in the then eight-year history of the ALC in which the school was asked to explain why a teacher had said or done something.

A wise person will be cautious about what he or she says about two subjects: Israel and the Syrian leadership. Although I've heard stories of the Mukhabarat trying to trap foreigners

with pointed questions, it has never happened to me nor to anyone I know. The new government is trying to improve its image in the world, and does not hassle foreigners, particularly those from Western countries.

LEGAL SYSTEM

Syria's system of justice is based on the French model. To hire an attorney, you must go to the Ministry of Justice and sign a power of attorney authorising him or her to represent you. Lawsuits and other civil cases may take years to settle. If you need an attorney, contact your embassy for recommendations; most lawyers speak English or French. Legal fees like most other expenses in Syria, are unbelievably low by Western standards: I hired an attorney to represent me in a lawsuit with a rental agent, and his retainer fee was only 1,000 SP (about US$ 20).

MONEY AND BANKING

Until the turn of the millennium there were no Western-style or private banks in Syria. The Commercial Bank of Syria (CBS) is a division of the government (banking was nationalised decades ago), and each branch has different functions. You need to go to one branch for a home loan, another for a savings account and yet another to cash a cheque. There are few chequing accounts in Syria, and some people here do not really understand what a cheque is. Unlike most other Arab countries, Syria has a cash economy. However, the CBS has recently embarked on a programme to make it more user-friendly and service-oriented, reducing the red tape and amount of time involved in completing transactions. There are also an increasing number of ATMs, and the bank is paying more interest on deposits than before. It has also issued a new Visa card that can be used for foreign currency.

There are, however, other options for banking in the major cities as there are an increasing number of foreign banks in Syria such as the Bank of Jordan and a new Islamic Bank (headquartered in the Gulf). The government has issued licenses for 10 new banks and expects to continue the process of opening up the banking system. You can also find international banks in both Beirut and Amman.

Currency Exchange

The fact that you cannot officially get foreign currency in Syria is a hassle, and you can withdraw only Syrian pounds at the ATMs. If you get paid in Syrian pounds and have no funds outside the country, you may have a problem paying bills at home or travelling to other countries because the pound is not worth much outside Syria. Lebanon and Jordan will convert some pounds to their own currency or US dollars, but usually at an unfavourable exchange rate. (You may also be able to spend Syrian currency in Lebanon.) Therefore, unless you get paid at least in part with foreign currency, make sure you have enough in a bank account outside Syria for debt payments and travel. You have to pay for air fares with hard currency unless you have an *iqaama* and can prove to the Commercial Bank that you get paid with pounds.

Few foreigners exchange funds at the official rate, because one can do it unofficially and gain 10–20 per cent. Cheques from embassies, national cultural centres and large companies operating in Syria are easily converted

THESE AREN'T BANKNOTES... THEY'RE SYRIAN FAST FOOD VOUCHERS

to pounds either officially or unofficially, but cash gets a better exchange rate. You might also have to get an official stamp from your embassy on the cheque; this is not a guarantee, but Syrians (especially the CBS) seem to view it as such. Once a merchant gets to know and trust you, you can sometimes use personal cheques drawn on foreign banks. Be careful about unofficial exchanges, though. It's still not entirely above board, and some expats have been cheated by strangers on the street. Know your moneychanger well.

It's best not to convert more hard currency to pounds than you need for short periods of time because if you need to trade it back for hard currency, you'll have to do it on the black market at an unfavourable rate. Bringing a supply of American one- and ten-dollar bills, for example, is a good idea. Most Syrians are happy to deal in US dollars. They come in especially handy in the souks.

Credit Cards

American Express, Visa and Mastercard are accepted by four- or five-star hotels, travel agencies and a few merchants who concentrate on sales to foreigners. Their primary use is to pay for luxury hotels and airline tickets, but note the following: if you have an *iqaama* but pay for your hotel with plastic, you will be charged an exchange rate that is approximately a quarter the official rate. This means that a room costing 2,000 SP in cash (about US$ 40) will cost about US$ 150 on your card. On the other hand, if you charge your airline tickets, you will get a discount from the cash price because the airlines have to convert cash payments to Syrian pounds at the official rate and want to avoid that. It's worth having a major card for this reason alone.

Local Bank Accounts

You may start either a Syrian pounds account or a hard currency account at the appropriate branches of the Commercial Bank as well as most of the new private banks. However—and this is important—if you deposit it in the CBS, you must declare the currency you want to deposit when you enter the country; if not, the bank will only allow you to withdraw pounds. You will be charged a fee every time you withdraw funds from the hard currency account, also, and you may not get regular account statements.

Only one expat I knew opened such an account, and she was unhappy with it because of the one per cent withdrawal fee and irregular statements.

The main method of keeping currency for both Syrians and foreigners has always been home hiding places or money belts worn under clothing, although that seems to be changing—at least for some foreigners and sophisticated Syrians—because of the new banking options. An additional drawback to banking your personal funds is the amount of time required for transactions; most branches are open only from 9 am to 1 pm, and it can take an hour to cash a cheque or withdraw funds. These things are changing with the opening of the banking system, but there's still nothing approximating the number and quality of banking services available in the West.

Foreign Banking Options

As mentioned above, you have two viable alternatives for banks out of the country: Lebanon and Jordan. Beirut is close to Damascus and has dozens of banks (some international) with Western-style services. Banking in Amman, Jordan, requires a two-day trip unless you take a service taxi before 7 am because the banks there close around noon and it's a 4- or 5-hour trip, thanks to the border crossing. Amman has a branch of Citibank as well as other foreign banks.

It is wise to bring a fair amount of cash to Syria unless your embassy or employer will cash cheques for you. Traveller's cheques are accepted by most hotels and travel agents, but you will have trouble using them elsewhere.

SHOPPING FOR BASICS

The nature of retail sales in Syria makes finding your daily needs time-consuming, but a bit less so than in the past because of some Western-style grocery stores that have opened. Some imported products can be found, but they often require a search and are expensive. Shopping hours are from around 9 or 10 am until 2 or 2:30 pm, then again from around 5 or 5:30 pm until 8, 9 or even 10 pm.

The majority of shops are Muslim-owned and are generally closed Fridays; Jewish shops are closed Saturdays and Christian shops on Sundays. Despite the general close down during the daytime on Fridays, a fair number of shops are open Friday evenings. There are also the options of Souk Al Jumaia (literally Friday Market) and the Baab Tooma and Baab Sharqi areas (*baab* is the Arabic word for gate) of the walled city. The latter two are predominantly Christian areas where shops are open on Fridays.

Some Sample Costs

You can live quite inexpensively unless you buy a lot of foreign products. For example, if you eat primarily local cuisine, you can get by on very little, as food prices are subsidised by the government, although this is changing too. Prices of selected local products, at this time, in Syrian pounds are given below:

- large rounds of fresh flat bread (each combined with *hommus*, *fool* or other dips large enough for one meal per person); 2-3 SP

- a half kilo each of *hommus*, *mtabbal* (an eggplant, yogurt and garlic dip) and *fool* (beans eaten for breakfast), enough for two meals for a small family; 60 SP
- a large loaf of French bread; 7 SP
- a whole roasted chicken, hot and ready to eat; 150 SP stuffed with rice and peas; 180 SP
- one kg of skinned, deboned chicken breast; 170 SP
- a *falaafel* sandwich (similar to a vegetable burrito); 20 SP
- a *shaawarma* (similar to a burrito with chicken/lamb); 30 SP
- locally brewed beer (half litre bottle); 20 SP
- one kg of tomatoes (in season); 20 SP
- one kg of potatoes or onions; 40 SP
- one kg of summer squash (in season); 15 SP
- a Syrian-made shirt or blouse; 800 SP and up
- Syrian-made snacks; 600–900 SP
- a Syrian-made coat; 1500 and up SP

There are a couple of things regarding prices you should be wary of. One is that even though the majority of shopkeepers are honest, there are those who try to overcharge foreigners. This is especially true for things without posted prices. Check prices in other shops, ask before you buy and pay attention to the change you get. The second price consideration is that items sold in bulk at large souks are quite a bit cheaper than the same product sold packaged at the fancier expat-oriented stores (and are fresher and of better quality as well). The local souks are the best way to go, for price, freshness and atmosphere.

Grocery Needs

Most of the locally grown produce is succulent in season. Peaches, cantaloupes, plums, tomatoes, cucumbers, pears, grapes and others are drenched with juice and have intense flavour. Chicken here is also very good and has little fat. Beef is not as good as in North America, and the lamb you buy from the butcher is not usually as tender and tasty as what you get in a restaurant. Lamb is the meat staple, and more expensive than beef or chicken.

The least expensive place to buy local food and household products such as laundry detergent and toilet tissue is in the small, ubiquitous neighbourhood markets. Many imported products are also available, but cost many times what they do in the export countries. For example, 500 grams of oatmeal imported from England costs over 175 pounds (US$3.50) at this time. A bar of Swiss chocolate costs the equivalent of US$3–4. The primary reasons for the price disparity between local and imported goods are heavy government tariffs on legally imported items, a robber-baron attitude on smuggled imports and price controls imposed on basic Syrian products, but not on imports.

If you wish to buy imported items, you generally have to shop at markets in the areas where most foreigners live—Abu Romaneh, Malki and Mezzeh. In the Abu Romaneh area, Nora, Badar, Sammar, Happy Family and Reddies groceries are sources; in Malki, a shop commonly called "the German Store" has many imports, including alcoholic beverages. In Mezzeh, most markets sell imported goods. Nora Grocery sells beer, wine, liquor, pork and fish—the latter two frozen.

A street-corner vendor selling a favourite Syrian treat—unripe almonds.
They are very sour, and are eaten with salt.

Crackdowns on smuggling make the availability of
imported items unreliable. Sometimes things such as
oatmeal and brown sugar can be found everywhere, but
then disappear for days or weeks. With the liberalisation
of the economy in general and the import/export business
specifically, there will no doubt be an increasing array of
foreign goods to buy in the future, but no doubt prices will
remain quite high.

Specialisation

Shops in Syria sell a narrow range of goods and are often
clustered into special souks. You go to a grocery store for
packaged goods, a fruit stand for peaches and apples, a
vegetable stand for carrots, one butcher shop for chicken
and another for beef, etc. There are four different types
of bakeries: one bakes only flat bread, a Syrian staple;
another bakes baguettes and sandwich rolls; a third creates
elaborately decorated European-style pastries; and the
fourth makes Syrian specialities—dense, rich confections
with heavy use of pistachios and sesame seeds. You
can find pork only at butcher shops in predominantly

Christian areas or at some grocery stores that cater to the expat community—or you can buy a whole pig from a Christian farmer! Even such things as turkey are available if you ask around. One year for Thanksgiving, a group of fellow teachers got together, found a turkey farmer, bought a turkey from him, and had a feast. It was, unequivocally, the tastiest and most tender turkey I've ever had!

A Rich History

A hundred years ago, the area now known as Sheik Muhiddeen was an old village on the side of Mt Qassion, separated from Damascus. It has mosques and other buildings that are centuries old, narrow, winding passages and colourful people.

In addition to larger shops, there are many street-corner kiosks that sell candies, toiletries, magazines, newspapers, etc. In some neighbourhoods you can buy fresh local produce from the farmers who trek through with their donkeys or horsedrawn carts, calling out their goods such as potatoes, pistachios, radishes and parsley. Buying all you can this way will save even more on your grocery bills, and it is convenient to have home delivery. There are juice shops everywhere, and 1.5 litres of freshly squeezed juice costs between 70 and 150 SP (US$1.40–3), depending on the type of fruit and the season.

In the central part of Damascus, Souk Al Jumaia in the Sheik Muhiddeen neighbourhood is a good place to buy bulk spices, herbs, dried beans, coffee and tea. The prices of fruits, vegetables and meats here are also the cheapest in Damascus, and the place is ripe with Arab character.

The area around Marjeh Circle and between there and Souk Al Hamidiyah are also good central shopping areas. And of course, the grand souk of the Arab world itself— Al Hamidiyah—has about every product you can find in Syria. Although the area officially called Souk Al Hamidiyah is only one street and its immediate side streets, the entire walled city is basically one giant souk.

The main daily shopping area for foreigners and wealthier Syrians in the central city is the Sha'alan area. This roughly fills the space between Mahdi Ben Baraki Street on the north, Maysaloun Street on the south, Abu Romaneh on the west and Salheeyeh Street on the east.

Here one can find the biggest selection of both imported and local products, although prices are often higher than at the souks previously mentioned.

Some Difficult Items to Find

Here are some common Western food and household goods that are difficult or impossible to find, and if available are very expensive. If you need any of the non-perishables, bring them with you:

- aspirin (bottled)
- barley
- broccoli
- cereals (hot)
- chocolate chips
- corn syrup
- cranberries
- grains (rolled)
- granola and muesli
- hair spray (pump type)
- molasses
- pet foods
- poppy seeds
- prunes
- pumpkin
- seafood (good quality)
- sausage (except local breakfast type)
- tampons

- bacon
- basil
- cat litter
- cheeses (hard)
- decaf coffee
- cornmeal
- ear plugs (you'll need these if noise keeps you awake)
- ham
- maple syrup
- Pepto Bismol or similar antacid (good for diarrhoea)
- prepackaged meals
- puddings
- sage
- sandwich meats (fresh)
- spray starch
- vitamin C tablets

If you have freezer space or the motivation for canning, it's worth preserving good summer produce for the leaner months of late winter and early spring when fruit and vegetable selection is poor, prices are high and the quality is not comparable to that of summer and autumn.

Other Options for Groceries

If you work for an embassy, you may have a commissary loaded with products from home. If not, you can buy almost anything in Beirut that you can in the West. Lebanon is

definitely the best shopping option for things not available in Syria.

Jordan also has much more available than it did 10 years ago, and an alternative in Amman is Safeway International. You can find several, though not all, of the products listed above at Safeway, and some imported items are cheaper than in Syria. If you live in Aleppo or Latakia, you can trek to Antakia in Turkey to find a wider selection of goods.

Food and Health Considerations

For me, one of the worst things about living in Syria was the often tainted food. Most Westerners—even people who have lived here and elsewhere in the Middle East for years —get occasional bouts of amoeba, worms, fungus or some combination of these. The reasons are the use of human wastes for fertiliser, and of contaminated surface water for irrigation and washing, and a general lack of consciousness about food hygiene. For eample, it is common to see large sheets of flatbread, hot from the oven, laid out to cool on dirty walls, fences and even steps.

A basket souk in Damascus.

Eat Fresh!

Avoid eating raw greens unless you soak them in bleach water (1–2 tablespoons of chlorine bleach for each gallon of water) for at least 20 minutes, then in fresh water for the same amount of time.

Drying parsley, mint, cilantro and other such herbs in the sun is also effective. Soak all fruits and vegetables in bleach water for 10–15 minutes, then in fresh water for the same amount of time before refrigerating them. Eggs are also dirty and should be washed with soapy water before using. Also, don't eat meat raw or rare; Syria is not the place for sushi or steak tartar, even if you could find them! A Syrian speciality that is exceptionally good is called *kibbeh*, made with either raw or cooked lamb. Avoid the raw variety. Flour is sometimes contaminated with insect and/or worm eggs (especially during late summer) and so should be kept refrigerated; it is wise to always sift or screen it before use. Wash the tops of cans before opening them. And finally, pick through all bulk items such as dried beans, rice, raisins and nuts for various indigestible items and occasional insects.

OTHER HOME PRODUCTS AND SERVICES

Specialisation is the rule with other products as it is with groceries. Paint shops don't sell electrical tape, electrical shops don't sell hammers and shops that sell door locks and screws don't sell paint. There is a special area in Souk Al Hamideeyeh for kitchen cookware. Mahdi Ben Barakee Street, near Arnoos Square, has kitchen and household shops that sell such things as vacuum cleaners and appliances, as does the street between the Parliament building and Al Maghribeeyeh Circle, where the palatial Commercial Bank headquarters is located.

The latter street and its side streets also have numerous hardware, paint and electrical shops. The major souk for electrical products (voltage regulators, fuses, fans, etc.) is near Marjeh Square. If you need tape, there is even a tape souk south of Souk Al Hamidiyah! Again, Sha'alan has a fair selection of most home products, but usually at higher prices than other locations.

Clothing, Linens, etc.

The biggest selection for modern clothing in central Damascus is in Sha'alan, Al Hamra Street, Salheeyeh Street and Marjeh Square. Tablecloths are everywhere—they're a Damascene speciality, but good towels, sheets and pillowcases are hard to find except at the fancier stores that cater to foreigners.

Locally made clothing is inexpensive, but generally of poor to moderate quality with the possible exception of Syrian-made denim products, which are heavy and well-made; I'm still wearing a denim shirt I bought there 14 years ago! Syrian shoes are very inexpensive but of poor quality and not available in long or narrow sizes. Despite the tremendous amount of cotton and number of sheep raised there, wool and cotton sweaters, cotton shirts (other than denim and dress shirts) and wool slacks are difficult to find. Most clothing seems to be made of rayon, called 'viscose'.

Computers

You can buy an increasing range of computer equipment but may have to pay a bit more than in Europe or North America.

If you need a computer, it might be best to buy the smallest, lightest package you can before moving to Syria. In the past, you also needed to bring batteries, print cartridges and any other accessories you might need for a computer, but that has changed. It still, however, might be wise to bring one of each accessory with you so you won't have to find a shop under pressure that sells your brand.

The Internet

By Western standards, it is not exactly easy to get online in Syria, but the Internet has become more popular and accessible throughout the country. In 2000, for example, only about 7,000 Syrians could access the Internet. However, that figure had skyrocketed to more than 240,000 by 2002. A 2007 look at a website called Arab0. com showed several dozen computer, data and information processing companies in Syria—a dramatic increase of such companies over just a few years before. Additionally, there are now numerous Syrian blogs, although some have access blocked or restricted by the government. The number of Internet cafés is growing all the time and usage of a terminal costs only 50 SP per hour. The number of providers in Syria is limited, however, so it is expensive to have your own; and at home, most connections are still dial-up, although this may change soon. Also, don't expect high-speed downloads! You can surf the web in Internet cafés or in larger public spaces such as Damascus' Assad Public Library and the Public Internet Hall. Syria is so intent on bringing its people up-to-speed with technology that the country even offers free computer training at about 100 locations.

Satellite TV

If you are a TV watcher, you will be much happier in Syria than you would have been over 10 years ago: at that time, there were only two channels available, both run by the government. But now, as mentioned earlier in this chapter, if you have a satellite dish, you can pay a monthly fee of around 1,300 SP and up for numerous international channels. The dish will cost you between US$ 100 and US$ 200 unless you can negotiate for your rental agent or landlord to provide one.

HEALTH AND MEDICAL
The cost of medical treatment in Syria may be the cheapest in the world. Pharmacies sell many prescription medications over the counter, so if you have a prescription from home and need a refill or know what you need, you can often just go to a pharmacist and buy it.

Insurance
If you want health insurance and can find an insurance company that sells portable policies (one that reimburses you for treatment in another country), I recommend it only for major medical procedures with a large deductible—something to help you in case of open-heart surgery or some other major medical requirement. I have not found an insurer in the United States that sells such policies, even with a deductible of several thousand dollars, but some British firms do. If you are American, before you buy, make sure the international policy covers medical treatment in the US too; some policies exclude treatment there because of the exorbitant medical costs.

A teacher I know who paid hefty premiums for three years never exceeded his annual deductible, even with the birth of a child and a family of six. I decided to forgo health insurance for myself and never regretted the decision.

Common Ailments
The most common illness affecting foreigners is amoebic dysentery, with intestinal worms perhaps running a close second. Colds and bronchitis are common, even in the heat of summer. Hepatitis is not as common, but still a problem, and a brief outbreak of cholera in the summer of 1993 was quickly stemmed, with the government designating specific clinics and hospitals for treatment to stop a potential epidemic.

If you have respiratory problems, they could be exacerbated by the often dirty air (usually in late summer and the coldest days of winter when there is no wind); but I have a strong allergy to dust as well as a moderate case of asthma and was bothered by neither—never even had to take any medicine for either while living there. The air quality in Damascus is growing worse, however, due to increasing industrialisation and number of automobiles. The biggest problems are dust during the long, dry summers, and soot from the kerosene heaters in the winter. Because of the intense dryness though, there's no problem at all with dust mites, so if you have an allergy for those, there is no need to worry about that.

Medical Costs

The average doctor's consultation fee at present costs only a few hundred pounds; a two-night stay for dysentery at the most expensive hospital in town cost me around 9,000 SP (US$ 180), and this included the doctor's fees and medicine. An ambulance ride costs only a few dollars. A bottle of Syrian-made cough syrup and a box of Syrian-made cough drops together costs less than 100 SP (US$ 2). Some doctors and pharmacists recommend imported medicine that costs several times more than an equivalent Syrian brand, but I have found little difference between local and imported varieties. Profit motive may be the main reason for pushing imported medicines, although educated Syrians in general have little faith in products made there.

Doctors and Dentists

There is no shortage of doctors in Syria: it seems there is one on nearly every block. Most have completed either medical studies or internships in the United States or Europe, and based on my experience, are as competent as North American doctors. They all speak a second language, usually English or French, and have office hours that roughly match those of businesses in general: from 8 or 9 am to 2 pm or so, then in the evening from around 5 pm until around 8 pm, Saturday through Thursday. Although dentists are not as plentiful as medical doctors, there are enough, their fees are low, and most of them also have Western training.

Hospitals

Most foreigners go to Shami Hospital, the newest and most modern facility and the one recommended by most Western embassies. It is the most expensive in town, but still costs only a fraction of what similar hospitalisation would cost in the United States. The Italian hospital is older and specialises in surgery. It is clean, seems fairly well equipped, offers good quality care and is less expensive than Shami. There is also a well-equipped hospital affiliated with Damascus University Medical School. There are small hospitals all over the city and even though they tend to specialise, you won't be turned away in an emergency.

For more complete medical information contact your embassy nurse or your employer.

Pre-arrival Inoculations

If you will be living in the cities in western Syria, you should get hepatitis A and B injections as well as update your polio and tetanus shots. Typhoid inoculation is also wise. Check with a travel clinic for more complete information.

MISCELLANEOUS
Laundry

There are many dry-cleaning and laundry shops where you can have clothes, carpets and other fabrics cleaned inexpensively. Be careful about valuable carpets and expensive clothing until you find a cleaner you can trust. Some expats take valuable fabrics to hotel cleaners because they think they do a better job.

Hairdresser

Barber shops and beauty salons are ubiquitous, and those that cater to foreigners and wealthy locals are often highly decorated, brightly lit and comfortable. Barbers and hairdressers usually do a good job, but a woman may have trouble getting them to do a simple job—they're accustomed to creating the elaborate hairstyles that so many young Syrian women seem to prefer. The cost at fancy shops is generally less than 500 SP (US$ 10). For men who wear their hair short and aren't fussy, barbers in the simpler shops used by most locals give decent cuts for around 100 SP.

Pets

If you bring a pet, you will have trouble finding food and cat litter. The only pet food that seems to be readily available is canned cat food at around US$1 per can. There are also not many veterinarians. Another problem with pets, especially larger dogs, is that there are no natural outdoor areas where they can roam. If you bring a cat that spends a lot of time outdoors, it might pick up diseases from and be terrorised by the cities' wild cats. I recommend leaving your pets at home with trusted friends or family. If you do bring them and have domestic workers, those workers can 'baby sit' the pets when you travel; this seems to be a common practice among embassy personnel.

The Physically Challenged

For those folks who may be wheelchair bound or who have other physical handicaps, life in Syria will likely not be pleasant. First, many older buildings have no elevators. Second, curbs have no ramps. Third, no toilets are equipped to assist the handicapped. And finally, crossing the street just about anyplace—even with a cane—would amount to suicide for a sight-impaired person.

FOOD AND ENTERTAINMENT

CHAPTER 6

'There is no love sincerer than the love of food.'
—George Bernard Shaw

SOCIALISING IS THE MAIN FORM OF ENTERTAINMENT for both Syrians and expats. Lunch and dinner with friends or extended families are often major social events, with restaurants full until after midnight, particularly on Thursday evenings (the 'weekend' in Syria is Friday).

DINING OUT

There is nothing that I would call 'gourmet' cooking in Syria; the local food is good but simple. There are countless restaurants, and most of them specialise in Syrian cuisine, serving food that ranges from just OK to wonderful. The number of stars displayed does not seem to indicate anything about quality, only price: I found that a five-star place usually served no better food than one with two-stars but may charge a lot more. Recently, though, some new restaurants serving foreign cuisine have opened, so the choices have expanded a bit.

You will find roughly the same items on the menus (if there are menus) in nearly all restaurants that serve Syrian food. The basics are *kabob* (grilled lamb) or *shishtaoo* (chicken), *kibbeh* (a delicious meat pie made with ground lamb, bulgur and seasonings), *boorak* (a cheese-filled pastry), various dips made from beans, seeds, yogurt, eggplant and hot peppers, the flat bread to eat the dips with, and various kinds of salads, including *tabouleh*, a Middle Eastern speciality. Many restaurants also serve *yalanji* (grape leaves stuffed with a spiced mixture of ground lamb and rice). The menu is essentially the same for breakfast, lunch and dinner, although there are a few things such as *fool* (fava beans cooked in oil, lemon juice and garlic, then topped with yogurt) and *fatteh* (a concoction vaguely similar to hot breakfast cereal) that are eaten only for breakfast.

In addition to whatever you order for lunch or dinner, you get a tray of pickles, olives and some raw vegetables. The Syrians always have tea or Arabic coffee after they eat. A meal that expands your belts to breaking point ranges in cost from 100 to 500 SP (US$ 2–10) per person, depending on the restaurant and what you drink. A few restaurants serve fish, but it is quite expensive and often not very fresh, except along the Mediterranean coast.

Only a few restaurants serve alcohol. Most teenagers will like this: soda drinks are immensely popular and Syrians drink them at all meals—even breakfast. The generic name for all soda here is 'cola', whether it's orange, strawberry or lemon-lime. If you order 'soda', you're likely to get a plate of grilled liver, since that's the Syrian word for liver!

Syrians love food that is either intensely sweet or sour. The country has one of the highest per capita consumptions of sugar in the world, and you may find the soft drinks to be the sweetest you've ever tasted. Even Coke, Pepsi and 7-Up that is bottled under license here is sweeter than it is in Greece, just a few hundred kilometres away. Syria's own brands are sweeter yet. The traditional Arab sweets, too, are so sweet they burned my palate. Conversely, the pickles are the sourest I've ever eaten. The natives also eat plain yogurt by the bowl and have a favourite drink, called simply *leban* (the Arabic word for yogurt) made from yogurt with a little water, salt and garlic added. Syrians eat a great deal of yogurt, believing it is good for the stomach. They also feel that garlic is an aid to health and digestion and can overcome stomach infections. Garlic, incidentally, is one of the main seasonings in Syrian cuisine, and it's used in copious quantities.

Here are some recommendations for excellent Syrian cuisine: Orient Club, across from the new Four Seasons Hotel—some people think that it offers the best traditional cuisine in the city; Abu al'Izz Restaurant in the ancient Souk Al Hamidiyah—old, dripping with atmosphere and often has live music; Nadil, near Baab Sharqi; Spicy, on the Abu-Romaneh side of Jisr al-Abiad—homemade-style Arab food; Haretna, Baab Touma area—great *mezze* (a group of dipping sauces for flat bread) and *kabobs*, and trendy and fashionable as well; and finally, for fish, there's a place called Bourj el-Roos that is quite rustic but cooks probably the best fish in Damascus—cheap, too.

Aside from Syrian cuisine, which varies a little by region, there are an increasing number of good restaurant choices. The Cham and Sheraton Hotels in Damascus have a Chinese and an Italian restaurant, respectively, but prices are nearly the same as what you'd pay in the United States or Europe, and the food is not great, in my opinion (but I think that's true of hotel food nearly everywhere). The luxury hotels have breakfast and lunch buffets. Some buffets are good, others not so special, but all are expensive.

There are several cafés that make fairly decent pizzas (although nothing like what you'd find in New York or Chicago), hot dogs and hamburgers, although I found them all to have a sweetness that seemed a bit out of place in such food. These places are most common in neighbourhoods where foreigners live and tourists go.

Several restaurants in Damascus bill themselves as French, but most I've tried serve food that's mediocre or worse: I've tried chicken cordon bleu at two of these, and it was the worst I've ever eaten; escargot at one was dry, tasteless and as rubbery as an old tire. The only things that make most of these restaurants French are the black-tie dress, the aloof attitude of the waiters and the high prices. One exception is a place in Damascus called Sindiana, on Mahdi Ben Baraki Street across from Subki Park. The food here is very good, but it's not for people on a tight budget: a meal with hors d'oeuvres and wine or imported beer can run the equivalent of US$ 20–30 per person. This would not be much for similar quality in North America or Europe but a whole family could have an excellent Syrian meal for the same price. Along with the hotel restaurants, Sindiana is an expat favourite.

Syrians relaxing over a water pipe at a typical cafe in the souk.

Here are some recommendations for non-Syrian cuisine and drinks: Sharia Medhat Pasha, at the turn to Baab Kisan—some folks think it serves the best pizza and pasta in Damascus, although service is often less than good and there's no menu, but just ask for whatever Italian dish you want and they will most likely be able to prepare it; Scoozi in Abu Romaneh—European-style café with great service; Il Circo in the Four Seasons—best wine selection and seafood in Damascus, but priced accordingly; Nadi al Sharq, Indian cuisine, and some say the best in Damascus; Vienna Café near the Cham Palace Hotel, opposite the Adidas store— makes dark bread sandwiches and apple strudel, among other things; Inhouse Coffee, a chain at the airport and other locations—great European-style coffee; Taj Mahal—Indian, of course; and The Swiss House—Swiss-style food, obviously.

In restaurants serving Syrian food, service is normally good, although waiters do not hang around your table. They put no pressure on you to hurry your meal, and when you want dessert, tea, coffee or the bill, you usually have to signal for the waiter.

Although dining out is enjoyable, especially in the summer when you can eat under the stars, there's a certain amount of Russian roulette involved. If you eat at restaurants regularly, you're bound to pick up occasional amoebas or worms; this happens a lot to some people, only rarely to others. You can lessen your chances of getting sick by avoiding restaurants that look dirty or whose waiters and cooks look like they spend little time on personal hygiene. Also, I recommend avoiding those with filthy toilets and washrooms.

Paying Up
To ask for your bill say, "*al hesab, min faddlak.*"

It's best to avoid uncooked greens and lightly-cooked or raw meat. Order your salads without lettuce and do not eat *tabouleh* except perhaps in late winter and early spring, after winter rains have flushed the soil. Also avoid the chopped mint and parsley garnishes sprinkled on most dishes. If you know you're susceptible to stomach infections, do not eat any raw vegetables or fruit you have not cleaned yourself.

A reasonable tip in Syria is around 10 per cent, although some Syrians tip less. It is also important to tip the bus boys. They don't share the waiter's tip, even though they do most of the work—waiters often only take your order, supervise the bus boys and assistants, give you your bill, and collect your money. Ten or fifteen pounds is an adequate tip for the bus boys.

Fast Food

There are now a handful of fast food franchises, including KFC (American fried chicken), Dunkin Donuts and a Finnish burger joint called Hezburger, the latter in the suburb of Dummar. No doubt there will be more to come, but many foreign residents are not happy with the invasion. There are delicious, cheap and (with the exception of the ice cream) healthier versions of Syrian 'fast food':

- *shaawarma* sandwiches made with lamb or chicken
- *falaafel* sandwiches
- juice shops that sell mixtures of milk and banana, strawberry, or other juices by the glass
- ice cream parlours that sell a multitude of pastries and ice cream treats

In areas where many foreigners live, there are also small cafés that sell Syrian-style (usually strangely sweet) hot dogs, hamburgers and pizzas to eat in or take out.

ENJOYING THE CULTURE/TRAVEL

CHAPTER 7

GEO MAGAZINE: What does it take to be a good traveller?
PAUL THEROUX: Courage. Curiosity. Travellers have to be
alone. They have to take risks. And they have to be among
things vastly different from those they have come from.
You see, a lot of people who travel are only looking for an
idealised version of home. They travel to find home with
better food, home plus more sunshine, home plus easier
parking, home plus no crime, home plus the possibility of
romance... They're not looking for the foreign, the strange,
the really outlandish... There have always been explorers,
and there have always been vacationers. The explorer has the
instinct to be the first person to see something, or the last.

COMPARED TO MOST OF THE WORLD'S CAPITALS, Damascus does not offer much in the way of the type of leisure activities that most Westerners are used to. If you are accustomed to regular artistic variety—everything from art to opera, music and cinema—life here will be a big adjustment, although there are more of these things available now than there were 10 years ago. Other Syrian cities have even less to offer. Still, if you look for and appreciate what there is, you can enjoy yourself. You can begin by not comparing lifestyles there to those in the West.

SEEING AND BEING SEEN

When Syrians walk around the streets and parks at night —something they do in hordes during nice weather—they wear their best clothing. Even conservative Muslim women often wear fashionable scarves and dresses. Young people parade around for a potential marriage partner, and the general milieu makes watching the locals an interesting pastime. People are also likely to strike up a conversation with you, maybe even invite you for tea or something to eat. In the summer, ice cream shops are particularly 'hot' places, much like the old soda shops in the United States.

SHOPPING

For most foreigners and for Syrians who have money to spend, this is a favourite pastime. For the locals, it is also part of night-time socialising; for people from the West, just experiencing the big souks is endlessly fascinating, often making the handicraft bargains one finds a secondary benefit.

A perfume shop at Souk Al-Hamidiyah; take note of the classical Damascene architecture with bands of different-coloured stone.

Jewellery

Gold and silver work is about the cheapest and most extravagantly designed anywhere. Meticulously filigreed bracelets, earrings, teaspoons and cocktail forks cost little more than the price of the gold or silver itself.

Handicraft Specialties

There are a number of handicrafts unique to Syria, if not in general appearance, at least in their particular patterns and details.

Brass and copper plates, bowls and pitchers are common and often lovely. The copper work is fast disappearing, though: it was a tradition of the dwindled Jewish population. The pieces are in high demand and prices are rising. Brass work, however, is still plentiful and relatively inexpensive.

Carpets, both old and new, locally made and imported from other countries of the region, are abundant. Bedouin carpets, in particular, are unbelievably cheap if you buy them in the desert. A caveat, though: be careful about cleaning them or getting them wet, as the dyes are sometimes not colourfast. One carpet I bought in the desert was totally ruined by massively bleeding colors when it got rained on!

In big souks you can find traditional garments such as dresses, capes, jackets and various sorts of gowns (for both men and women) with a big variety of embroidery. Tablecloths and pillowcases with unique Damascene designs are now made by machines but are still striking and inexpensive. There is a special brocaded fabric known as damask, named for Damascus; you can buy this by the yard, and have a tailor (also inexpensive) make whatever you want with it.

Another Syrian specialty is mosaic woodwork. There are two basic types: one uses thin layers of assembly-line veneers; the other has each piece of wood, bone or mother-of-pearl cut and set by hand. The latter are more costly than veneered pieces but are still a very good buy.

There is wide variation in the quality and design of mosaics. Some workmanship is crude, while some is very nice. Some inlays only have different-coloured woods, while others contain bone or mother-of-pearl (most of it artificial). You can find boxes of every shape and size, trays, tables, game boards ranging from lap-size to large table-top models, and even desks made from mosaic.

Yet another Damascus speciality is handblown glass. Across the street from Baab Sharqi is one glass factory; another is in the handicraft souk mentioned earlier. Both factories ('factory' is a bit misleading—these are small shops) make glass in three different colours: cobalt blue, green and amber-brown. Each colour is produced for a month, another colour for another month, etc. The objects range from small tea glasses (the traditional way of drinking tea) and small bowls to large, garishly painted vases, light fixtures and water pipes for smoking called 'hubble bubble'. In between are various sizes of bowls, glasses, cups, ashtrays and decorative pieces. You can either buy off the shelf or specify what you'd like, and they'll make it for you. I had a half-dozen tea glasses specially made; they were ready the next day and cost the equivalent of US$ 0.50 each.

Finally, antiques are available, some extraordinarily wonderful, some interesting, others just old. But again the prices are low compared to items of similar age and quality in North America or Europe. You can find things ranging from miniature filigreed birds to Bedouin knives and jewellery to large pieces of furniture inlaid with silver and mother-of-pearl.

Bargaining

Prices on food items are usually not negotiable, but you can bargain on handicrafts. Most merchants expect it. This Middle Eastern way of business almost resembles a game of wits, such as chess or checkers. Although it involves some drama and quick thinking, it is always a friendly exchange—another way to promote social interaction and cooperation. Once you get a feel for the going prices on things, you'll be able to tell which items have reasonable prices and which prices are too high.

CINEMA, THEATRE, CONCERTS, GALLERIES
Cinemas

Except for an occasional good Hollywood production (usually appearing a year or two years after its United States release) cinemas here are the haunting grounds of rowdy young men watching Egyptian soap operas or super-violent American and Asian movies. When a good film appears, it's usually been cut, often poorly, by the censors. An exception to this situation is the international film festival, in late October and early November, and the usual showings at the Cham Palace Hotel cinema. The festival films are shown at both Cham Hotel cinemas, the Al Hamra Street Theatre and a couple of other locations. The movies at the festival are predominantly from the region—India to North Africa and southern Europe—and most have either English or French subtitles, while the usual fare at the Cham Hotel cinema is Western films of the same kind and quality you might see at a large cineplex in the US—although several months later.

Music

Music is an integral part of Syrian life. It sets the mood in the background to almost every situation. As you travel through the country, you will hear a range of Middle Eastern tunes in the souks, cafés and various businesses. In the morning, you will most likely hear the slow, sleepy sounds of popular musicians, while the more hectic afternoons call for livelier, more percussive beats

Although Syria ostensibly protects intellectual property, pirating of brand names in general, music and video in particular, are widespread. Audio and video tapes, CDs and DVDs in Syria are often pirated. Those whom this does not offend ethically take advantage of the situation to build their music library. Some shops buy good quality tapes or CDs and record onto them from compact discs, selling the copies for less than 200 SP, and the sound quality is excellent. (Remember, however, that no royalties are paid to the copyright owners. It's also worth bearing in mind that, should customs inspectors in the U.S. or European countries find the bootleg discs or tapes, they will likely confiscate them.) Just about all popular music in the Western world and from Arab musicians is available. Alternative rock is rare and blues and jazz selections are limited, however.

Some shops sell traditional Arab music instruments —including handmade ones—as well as electric guitars, modern drums, etc.

Video Cassettes, DVDs and CDs

An NTSC VCR from North America will be of little use in Syria, since the videos used there will not play on them. Get a multi-system VCR from Lebanon (mine, an Akai that played NTSC, Pal and Mesecam tapes, cost around US$ 300) and hope you land an apartment with a TV that will also accommodate other systems. DVDs have not yet replaced videos to the extent they have in the West and Japan, but their presence is increasing. Again, though, DVDs have 'area codes' that make them unplayable in machines not made for those codes, so if you take a DVD player, make sure it has the capacity to play all codes—or at least those of the Middle East and Europe.

If you work for the US Embassy, American Language Centre or Damascus Community School you can check out tapes and DVDs from the extensive library stocked by USIS (US Information Service); if you work for the Canadian

Embassy, you can get those from their Chimo Club; the Australian Embassy also had them available. You can also rent local videos (Pal system) and DVDs for the equivalent of about US$ 0.50 each. Before you jump for joy, I must tell you that they are often copied from copies which were copied from copies who knows how many times, making the quality of both sound and picture poor. Still, they're a bargain, and as with many other things in Syria, you'll adjust.

Live Theatre

Except for an occasional international school production, theatre is sparse: it is not at all part of traditional Middle Eastern culture. Syria, however, has two national theatre groups, and a large and lovely new national theatre has been built in Damascus. This will hopefully improve the choices for live performances. Live shows are also held at the Al Hamra Street Theatre.

Concerts

There are quite a few concerts, ranging from classical European and classical Arab to American jazz and Indian music. These are performed at the cultural centres (including the Arab Cultural Centre in Mezzeh), at the Al Hamra Street Theatre, at the Asad library, in hotel ballrooms and at the new performance hall at the Ebla Cham Hotel about halfway between the airport and Damascus. For information regarding concerts, keep your eyes open for notices posted in schools, embassies and cultural centres. *The Syria Times*, Syria's English language newspaper, often gives notices of art exhibitions and dance and musical performances. Concerts are sometimes sponsored by an embassy and you can ask to have your name added to the list of people who receive invitations. It helps if you can read Arabic, because performances not geared toward the expat community are often advertised only in Arabic.

The Syrian National Symphony performs two annual concerts at the Ebla Cham performance hall. Get information about and tickets for these from the Conservatory of Music near Al Omayyad Circle.

Art Galleries

Although the arts in Syria are anything but avant garde, there are several shops in the Sha'alan area of Damascus that sell paintings and drawings. They have some nice work, some of which catches the essence not only of Damascus, but of Arab culture and place in general. Prices are low by Western standards. Also there is a painter named Nazir who has his own shop (in the city's Jewish quarter) jammed full of his paintings, which range from so-so to very nice; some are quite traditional, others unusual, but most all include some form of human heads. His prices are very low. He also makes all his own paint, brushes, paper, etc. "as a link to artists of the past", he says.

Mustafa Ali's Gallery is also located in the Jewish quarter of the Old City. He's an internationally known Syrian sculptor who is trying to turn the dilapidated buildings of the Jewish quarter into a bohemian art district. Head north from Straight Street, running through the Old City, and locals can guide you to this area.

In addition to the commercial galleries, Damascus has several public galleries, most of them centrally located. Exhibitions change frequently and include artists from the region and sometimes Europe. Check the *Syria Times* or the galleries for information. The various countries' cultural centres also occasionally sponsor art and photography exhibits.

Other Performances

Suppose you're walking home late one night, and you hear the sounds of a drum, clapping and chanting male voices. You look for its source and see a man or two leading the chants, white skullcaps on their heads, standing on the shoulders of others who are walking in circles. You have just encountered a traditional Muslim wedding party. While the men are doing this ritual in the street, the women are in a nearby restaurant or home dancing, singing and feasting. When the women finish eating the men will eat, and the party will last most of the night.

Each September an international festival is held in Bosra, in its amazingly well preserved Roman amphitheatre. The

The still-used Roman amphitheatre in Bosra seats 15,000 people.

festival runs every night for approximately three weeks and has many international folk dance and music groups. If you're there during the day (hotel rooms are hard to find, since Bosra is a small town), you can also witness rehearsals. There are also occasional folk dance and music festivals in Palmyra, Aleppo and other cities.

Finally, just prior to the Bosra festival, there is a regional festival of sports, music, dance—just about everything—at the sports city north of Latakia on the Mediterranean coast.

ODDS AND ENDS

When entertainment is limited, you can sometimes find it in places you wouldn't think of at home.

Enjoying the History and Culture

When you live in a country with such a broad variety of cultures and immensely rich history, learning about and enjoying these things seems as natural as eating.

Damascus is possibly the oldest continuously inhabited city on Earth; it's so old that its earliest date of settlement is not known, but it was mentioned in Egyptian writing around seven millennia ago as Damashq—its present name in Arabic. Aleppo was established around 5,000 years ago, and Latakia was built in the 24th century BP by the Greek Seleucos Nicator. Damascus and Aleppo in particular have vast numbers of interesting buildings, remains and diverse neighbourhoods: the Omayyad Mosque, Azem Palace (an Ottoman treasure), museums and souks are only the best known.

Some of the neighbourhoods of Syrian cities look as they did hundreds of years ago except for the motor vehicles and some Western dress. A perceptive person will delight in the variety of the oldest neighbourhoods, whether Christian, Muslim or Jewish. A good pair of walking shoes and a desire to lose yourself in other worlds are the only requirements for hours of enjoyment. The ability to read and speak Arabic even moderately will enhance the experience, helping you read signs and dates on buildings and talk to the local residents whose families may go back hundreds of years in the same spot—even the same house.

Another thing I highly recommend—although not entertainment, as such—is to learn about Islam and experience some of it first hand. With the great antagonism that has in some ways always existed between 'the children of the book' (as Muslims call themselves, Christians and Jews), and the more recent escalation of that antagonism, it would do people of all three religions good to not only learn more about the others but to experience some of them. For example, I attended Friday prayers at two different mosques while living in Syria, one of them the grand Omayyad Mosque, the other at a Shi'a mosque where the attendees were predominantly Iranian. The latter particularly left a great impression on me for the fervency with which they prayed. Anyone can attend prayers, but unless you are Muslim and know the routines and etiquette, I recommend not doing it alone so as to avoid making serious faux pas and thereby increasing the misunderstandings and suspicions among us. In both cases, I asked Muslim acquaintances if they would mind my going along with them to experience Friday prayers at those mosques, and in both cases, they were both surprised and delighted that I had asked. In the Shi'a mosque, I detected what I perceived as some

hostility toward my presence (although my reading could have been wrong), but no one was rude or threatening to me in any way. At the Omayyad Mosque, I not only didn't feel any hostility, but after the service, several people approached me and asked if I was Muslim, and if not, why was I there, where was I from, etc. When I (with the help of some interpretating from the acquaintance I was there with) told them that, no, I was raised as a Christian but wanted to experience the Muslim way of worship and try to understand their beliefs more, their responses were all very positive and welcoming.

The Media

Until January 2001, all Syrian media was strictly controlled by the Ba'ath Party. In November 2000, President Bashar al-Asad gave political parties the right to publish in an attempt to further loosen the government's authoritarian hold. In January 2001, the Communist party's *Sawt al-Shaab* (People's Voice) became the first newspaper in 30 years not printed by the Ba'ath party or government.

In spite of this major step toward freer speech, however, the paper will probably not challenge the leadership since the Communist party is part of the National Progressive Front, a group of seven parties dominated by the ruling Baa'th Party. Still, it is an important first step and a telling gesture.

There are several Arabic language newspapers available from most countries of the Middle East. *The Syria Times* used to be predominantly filled with propaganda about the wonderful leadership of President al-Asad, but it recently has increasing news from international presses, some sports and information about local artists and artistic events, and other valuable info. It also lists emergency phone numbers and other miscellaneous information.

Foreign newspapers such as the *International Herald Tribune*, *The New York Times*, *The Wall Street Journal* and *Le Monde* are available as well as magazines such as *Time*, *Newsweek* and others from Britain and France. All of these are several days old when they hit the newsstands, and occasionally have pages removed if the material is considered either too sexually explicit (an article about Madonna was cut from one magazine and one about Israel from another), critical of Syria or favourable to Israel.

For TV, there's an option of a satellite dish and programmes. Check the info in Chapter 5 for that.

There are a few radio channels available in AM, FM, medium wave and short wave, but most of these are Arabic stations with little or no variety. You can pick up Voice of America, the BBC, and a few other outside channels if you are in certain locations and have a medium and short wave receiver.

Bars and Clubs

Although there are only a handful of bars or nightclubs in Syria (almost all of them in Damascus), the Canadian and British diplomatic personnel have clubs that are open to expats who work for their embassies or for foreign businesses or cultural centres and have *iqaamas*. Syrians are not allowed nor are foreigners who are domestic employees. You must be invited by a British expat to go to the Pig and Whistle on Tuesday nights, and the Chimo Club (Canadian) is open every other Friday evening. These clubs open around 5:30–6 pm and close before 10 pm. In addition, there is a place called The Night Club in the Sha'alan area that has live Arabic music, and a club called The Piano Bar near the entrance to Baab Sharqi. The latter admits only couples.

Believe it or not, there are genuine burlesque clubs in Damascus. One, called The Crazy Horse Club, is near the Cham Palace Hotel and across from the Syrian military officers' club. There is another, called The Chicken Club, near by. These clubs are open all night, and are rumoured to be pick-up spots for prostitutes.

Some other recent additions to clubs are: Mar Mar, near the Bakri baths in Baab Touma—the owner performs with his own funk band regularly; Domino, a bar and café in Baab Touma, the heart of the Christian centre in the Old City—becomes a disco after 11 pm; Backdoor, at the Barada Sports Club in Mazrah—a trendy dance hall for R&B and Arab pop, with an entrance fee of 1,000 SP, a fortune by Syrian standards.

Exercise

Expats can work out at a health club called Club al-Droubi in Abu Romaneh (a block from the Saudi Embassy) and another in Mezzeh. The major hotels also have health clubs, and the Cham Hotel has the only bowling alley in Syria.

The Hash House Harriers sponsors several events each month (usually on Fridays) for running, hiking and camping in addition to some social activities. The Damascus Community School compound has a running track that can be used by its teachers, teachers at the American Language Centre, and employees of the American Embassy before 8 am and after 3:30 pm on school days and all day on weekends.

It is not safe to run or cycle on most streets in Syrian cities, except on Fridays, because of the traffic and the road and sidewalk hazards, but there are areas in the mountains around Bludan and Maalula as well as in the desert where you can hike. Don't get close to military installations, though, and carry a few large stones to chase off the unpredictable half-wild dogs if you're in the desert.

During the summer, you can cool off in a number of swimming pools. Most are on the outskirts of the city and cost only 150 SP (US$ 3) or so to use. The pools at the Sheraton and Meridien Hotels in Damascus are also open to the public, but cost around 400 SP (US$ 8); they are favoured by rich local young people and foreigners who can afford the US$250-a-night rooms. You can purchase health club memberships at most luxury hotels.

The cities have several old—some ancient—Turkish baths, some with masseuses, but of course, for men only.

Expat Organizations and Cultural Centres

The associations for American, British and Canadian women have libraries and video cassette access, and sponsor entertainment such as lectures, folk dances and musical performances. The American Women of Damascus (AWD) meets monthly from September to June; subgroups of this organisation for gardening, cooking and other interests meet whenever the group decides. Foreign cultural centres also have libraries and sponsor musical events and lectures.

THINGS NOT AVAILABLE

If you're an avid golfer, hunter, or fisherman, you will be disappointed: Syria offers none of the above. Although some Syrians hunt animals in the desert or birds just about any place outside the cities, foreigners cannot carry guns. The only golf course is a tiny one for guests at the Ebla Cham Hotel.

HOLIDAYS AND CELEBRATIONS

Most holidays are quite subdued. There are lots of government-related holidays, the big ones sometimes accompanied by fireworks exploded on Mt. Qassioun. Some have parades, military aircraft buzzing the city and party speeches, but the celebrations seem staged.

Christmas is celebrated in the Christian communities, and there are two Easters—one for Eastern, one for Western Christians. These days of Christian celebration are also official holidays with schools and government offices closed, but most shops open.

The Two Eids

The truly big celebrations are Islamic: the two three-day holidays called Eid. The first, Eid al-Fitr, immediately follows the fast during the Islamic month of *Ramadan*. During

Ramadan, you may be invited to eat with a Muslim family and experience the evening meal, called *iftar*, that breaks the day's fast.

Food is set on the table in vast quantities (none of them have eaten or even drunk water since dawn), and the family is seated and ready to attack the food at the broadcasts from the minarets that mark the end of the day's fast. Once the eating starts, no one says anything for a while, and unlike the regular meals that often drag on for an hour or more, the food is gone in minutes! Most men and even quite a few women visit the mosques for the special prayers after *iftar* every evening.

After Ramadan ends, Eid al-Fitr begins, and people gorge themselves on special foods, stay up all night and spend all their spare time visiting extended families and friends. It is a custom for children to get money from their uncles. For a poor uncle in a typically large Syrian family, this can be a problem! There are also carnival-type rides set up in large parks for kids, and young people ride horses and go-carts in and around some parks.

The second Eid, called Eid al-Adha, is celebrated in about the same manner and follows the traditional end of *Hajj*, the pilgrimage to Mecca. The night before this feast begins there's a buzz of activity everywhere and great excitement in the air. The souks and shops stay open until midnight, and practically everyone stays out late shopping for special foods and gifts. Don't be surprised if you see a camel's head and sheep's testicles—considered delicacies—displayed in the butchers' stalls. It is a happy time. People are in good spirits and you will hear a great deal of laughter, joking and sometimes women's singing. Women get their hands hennaed in the courtyards of the mosques, while men huddle in groups to discuss the day's events and children run and play everywhere. The mosques are also crowded with the faithful.

During this feast, Muslims who can afford to do so, traditionally slaughter an animal and donate its meat to the poor. If you are out on this day, you will probably cringe as you see many sheep, lambs and goats awaiting their fate. On the first morning of the feast, the sidewalks in some areas are often stained with blood.

Most Westerners are spared the reality of where their meat comes from, but in the Middle East, it's all out in the open. During both Eids, almost nothing is open, government or private, the streets are nearly deserted night and day (except around the parks), and it is the only time the city streets are peaceful and quiet. It is also difficult to find daily needs during Eid, although some Jewish and Christian shops are open. It's best to stock up on basic needs before the holidays begin.

The dates for Eid are determined by lunar criteria and so occur at different times in each Islamic country and each year. Even though it is officially only three days, if those days fall mid-week some shops, schools and embassies close for the entire week. People who can afford to do so often leave town for a week.

If you decide to travel anywhere in an Islamic country during either Eid, make sure you have reservations. Rental cars vanish as quickly as hotels, buses and local airlines fill up. Whatever transportation is available during this time will probably cost you two or three times as much.

DOMESTIC TRAVEL

For many of us who live or have lived in Syria, being able to travel in the country and region is one of our greatest joys. Even people who are familiar with the area's history are surprised at the ancient treasures they can find, many of them unfamiliar even to most Syrians. The country has more than 200 historical and archaeological sites from as far back as 7,000 years ago and most are within a day's trip from Damascus. And unlike Europe, Egypt and Turkey where ruins are overrun with tourists, sometimes roped off for protection from wear and tear or vandalism, all but the most well-known sites in Syria are usually deserted, although not quite as much as they were in the past. This isn't a guide book, but I want to point out some highlights.

Eastern and Central Syria

Following the Euphrates River from the Iraqi border in the southeast to the dam near Aleppo in the north, you'll find remnants of several different civilisations.

At Doura Europa, the remains of a city built 2,500 years ago by Alexander the Great on the Euphrates near Iraq, my partner and I saw one lone backpacker from Switzerland and one couple from elsewhere in Europe. It was just us, the fantasy of history and a sandstorm blowing in from Iraq that turned the sky yellow and added to the mystique of the experience.

We spent a full day climbing and exploring Halabeeyeh, the ruins of a Roman outpost on the Euphrates north of Deir ez-Zor, and saw no one except a couple of shepherds on surrounding hills; the only sounds were those of the wind, the distant tinkling of sheep bells and the thump-thump-thump of irrigation pumps on the river. Shards of pottery were everywhere, ranging in age from Roman to early Muslim.

South of Raqqa, on the Euphrates in north-central Syria, are the ruins of an ancient walled city a long way off the highway but with a serviceable road leading to it.

The entrance arch and grand promenade at Palmyra.

In the central deserts there are ruins of Arab castles, some that you must drive across roadless desert to reach (make sure you rent a four-wheel drive if you plan to go to these). These, too, are virtually deserted except for an occasional Bedouin and his sheep. The best preserved of these is called the Eastern Palace and is about halfway between Palmyra and Deir ez-Zor. The most magnificent ruins in this part of the country are those of Palmyra, the Roman city that was last ruled by Queen Zenobia, who was Syrian and is a heroine to most Syrian women. For me, there is something surrealistic and intriguing about this place and what I call "the valley of the dead"—a valley northwest of Palmyra where Roman aristocrats were buried in caves and funerary towers, a few of which are still in fairly good condition. On the southern edge of the ruins is an oasis (the source of water for Palmyra) where you can walk between the winding adobe walls surrounding date and olive groves that are centuries old. And on a hill overlooking the Roman ruins are the ruins of a 12th or 13th century Arab castle that you can tour for a small fee—with a local Bedouin guide.

The far northeastern corner of the country does not hold as much visible historical interest but is culturally diverse. This is the Kurdish area of Syria, and some enclaves of people here speak the ancient language of Syriac.

In addition to the historical wonders of the desert, the steppe and the Euphrates, cultures and handicrafts are quite diverse, and noticeably different than in the cities to the west. Deir ez-Zor has the largest souk in eastern Syria, and the prices are lower than those in Damascus. In Tadmor, the desert town at Palmyra, shops sell both new and antique Bedouin goods; but look around before you buy, because the prices vary quite a bit from shop to shop. Palmyra is the most popular and well-known tourist site in Syria.

You might notice that people along the Euphrates are less cordial than those in Damascus, but some are still friendly. Most people here are quite dark-skinned and wear a wide variety of clothes—especially the women. More women also wear veils and cover their heads than they do in the big cities to the west.

The desert people are mostly Bedouins whose insulated culture goes back thousands of years and who will find you as fascinating as you find them. In the spring the steppes and deserts are dotted with the rectangular, black goatskin tents of the Bedouins.

The Population Centre Corridor

Along the main highway between Jordan and Turkey, there is a vast array of interesting sites. Bosra, in the south, has perhaps the world's best-preserved Roman amphitheatre, an impressive structure that seats 15,000 people and is still used regularly. It is even more special with the Muslim citadel, about 900 years old, built around it.

A Muslim village was constructed at the same time as the citadel among the ruins of the Roman city surrounding the coliseum. Pieces of columns and other debris from Roman structures were incorporated into the walls of the Muslim town. It is still inhabited and mostly unchanged for the last half-dozen centuries, creating alluring juxtapositions. There is a mosque, for example, built with columns taken from the

The sculpture garden above the Roman amphitheatre in Bosra.

Giant water wheel at Hama.

Roman amphitheatre, remains of a rare round cathedral, and the remains of a church in which the priest purportedly told Mohammed that he would be the next prophet.

Some way north of Bosra is the village of Shahba, the birthplace of Philip, a Roman emperor from 1763–1758 BP. Here are more Roman ruins, including some well-preserved mosaics in a museum.

North of Homs is the city of Hama with its giant old water wheels on the Orontes River. Near Hama is what's left of Apamea, a third century Greco-Roman city that had half a million inhabitants. Near Aleppo are ghost towns, the remains of the Roman road that ran from Turkey down to the Red Sea, and Ebla, a tell discovered in 1974 with records of human habitation from 4500 BP.

Atop a hill in Aleppo is an enormous citadel that helped the Muslims defend their territory from the Crusaders. (Aleppo is called Haleb in Arabic—a variation of the word for milk, so named because Abraham purportedly milked his goats on the hill where the citadel now stands.) This is Syria's second-largest city and is full of other interesting things to see and do, including a great souk (12 kilometres or 7 miles under one roof) that sells its own distinctive handicrafts, a huge mosque and a good museum.

Along this north-south route there is much more than ruins to see. Near Der'a on the Jordanian border there are waterfalls, one of which disappears into a spectacular, rugged canyon. The area in the southeast of Syria is also heavily volcanic in origin, and there are vast fields of lava rock and numerous cinder cones.

North of Damascus are several monasteries, convents, and predominantly Christian villages with lovely churches. Sydnaya, the largest and most beautiful of the convents, sits high on the side of a desert mountain, with a village wrapped around its base. You can stay overnight here for a token charge and enjoy the dramatic view across the desert. Maalula, an ancient Aramaean village north of Sydnaya, has caves where early Christians hid, and many older people here still speak the language Christ spoke. Some houses built on the cliff in this town incorporate some of the caves as rooms.

In Maalula, some houses incorporate the caves in which the early Christians lived.

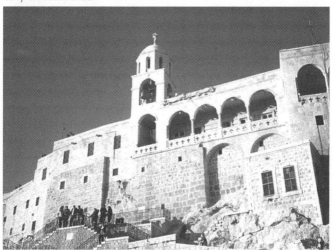

The convent at Sydnaya, in the mountains north of Damascus.

Art gallery in cave at monastery of Marmoosa.

In the desert northeast of Nabk, about 113 km (70 miles) from Damascus, is a small monastery called Marmoosa that you must walk about 2 km (a little more than a mile) to reach. It has a spectacular setting, built as it is on the foundation of a Roman guard tower at the opening of a canyon that drops precipitously to the desert floor. Overnight guests are welcome here for a small donation of food or cash or some volunteer work in excavation and restoration. The monastery's chapel was built 1,300 years ago, and its frescoes were painted in the 11th century, then the structure was abandoned for hundreds of years. Father Paulo of Marmoosa, originally from Italy, speaks fluent Arabic and good English. The isolation of this place is wonderful, especially after living in a noisy city. You can sit outside in the evening, watch the sun set across the desert valley, then enjoy an astounding display of stars after dark. The accommodations are rustic, the food basic, but the experience cannot be equalled. It also features a unique gallery—in a cavern—of a series of paintings that illustrate a story about the death of a group of people here in ancient times.

The Coast and Mountains

When it's hot and humid at the coast, and hot and dry in the desert, the coastal mountains are a welcome retreat. There is actually a double spine in this range, with the westward one being lusher, wetter and cooler than the one to the east.

Multiple ruins exist along the coast and in the mountains, mostly Crusader castles. One of the world's oldest sites of civilisation is just north of Latakia: Ugarit, called Ras Shamra in Arabic. The tell here contains several layers of successive civilisations. The last pre-Arab dwellers were Greek fishermen who some 2,000 years ago built a small fishing village atop the mound, apparently oblivious to what lay beneath them. One of the world's earliest alphabets—one that used cuneiform symbols—was discovered at this site, as well as Egyptian hieroglyphics and Sumerian, Hittite and Babylonian texts. Ugarit has only been partially excavated but is an interesting place to spend a day. The museums in Damascus and Aleppo contain some of the treasures found here.

A ancient funerary tower in a valley north of Palmyra.

The best-known and best-preserved crusader castle guarded a gap in the coastal mountains between what is now Homs and Tartus on the Syrian coast. Its French name is Krak des Chevaliers, its Arabic name Qalaat Al Hosn. It is massive. North of here are several other castles, each with its own distinction.

Many of the mountain villages are lovely places where you can have lunch and enjoy the natural beauty; some of them have crafts markets where you can find things unique to that particular village or area. Also, the terraced hillsides, olive orchards and extensive vineyards provide an aura of bucolic timelessness.

The farther north you travel in the mountains, the higher and lusher they become. Kassab, in the far northeastern corner, sits in mountains that seem more like northern Greece than the Middle East. This area is predominantly Armenian-Syrian, descendants of Armenians who came to hide from Turkish purges. This is a rural area of apple orchards, grapevines, wild figs, pomegranates and thick pine forests. The culture is quite different from the rest of Syria, and there are obvious clues to that difference: most of the people do not look Arab; signs are written in both Arabic and Armenian; and there are many churches and monasteries but few mosques. Syria's most beautiful and cleanest coastline is also near here.

GETTING AROUND

You can get by with public transportation anywhere in Syria, but in the central and eastern parts, a car is desirable; bus and taxi service is limited and it is possible to get stranded in remote places. Damascus has dozens of rental agencies including a few international franchises such as Budget, Avis, Hertz and Eurocar, all with branches at the airport. Rental costs are similar to anywhere in the world, ranging from around US$ 30 (sub-compact) to US$ 80 (luxury) per day. (NOTE: You cannot take a Syrian rental car out of the country.) All you need to rent a car is your passport, an international driver's licence, and a cash or credit card deposit of US$ 500–1,000 or as much as 50,000 SP (US$ 1,000). Before you rent, find out what form of payment the agency requires; some will only accept hard currency or credit card, even if you have an *iqaama*.

Gasoline stations are quite difficult to find inside the cities —there are still no private oil companies, no rotating Shell or Union 76 signs, but they are plentiful along the major highways in the western part of the country. If travelling through the desert or steppes, you may not see one for a hundred kilometres or more. In rural areas, though, you can always ask around (in Arabic)—as I once had to do while driving along the northern coast—and will usually find someone with containers of gas who will sell you some gasoline (*banzine* in Arabic). Prices are regulated by the government—currently around 25 SP per litre—so don't be conned into paying more, unless you want to pay a bit extra for bothering a local resident. If you stop at a fuel pump that does not have a working gauge, ask for a specific number of litres, then only pay for that amount.

When driving, you must follow the rules of the open road. Syrians drive anywhere and everywhere on the highways, just like they do the cities, so don't assume you can drive absentmindedly on divided highways—you might meet a loco taxi driver coming over a rise, headed the wrong way on your side of the road. Also, it is not rude to honk your horn or flash your lights before you overtake another vehicle: in fact, it is expected that you will announce your intention of passing, and you may have to do so to get a driver to pull over. Likewise, if someone comes flying up behind you with lights flashing and horn honking, move over quickly—this is also expected. Finally, driving at dusk and dawn is maddening as few drivers turn their lights on until complete darkness. This means coming over a hill and finding yourself nose-to-tail with a slower-moving vehicle sans lights, or nose-to-nose with an oncoming driver, passing in your lane with no headlights. Drivers apparently think it is safer to drive with lights off, constantly flashing them to announce their presence. The highway between Homs and Damascus at night resembles an endless string of migrating fireflies!

If you do not drive or prefer to be driven, the cheapest transportation option is the government-operated intercity bus system called Karnak, named after the famous Egyptian temple in Luxor. You can travel from one end of the country to the other for nearly nothing, and the buses are reasonably comfortable, provided you can put up with cigarette smoke thicker than the proverbial London fog. Unlike the general Arab disregard for time, however, Karnak is on schedule most of the time.

Another option is an intercity taxi, called service taxi, which is only a little more expensive than Karnak, and you must try one at least—they provide an unequalled cultural experience. The cars are big and old American land yachts, many so banged up and pathetic-looking you wonder how they make it between cities, but they do. It is rare to see them broken down, so Syria must have some of the world's best mechanics to keep these dinosaurs running—parts have not been made for 1952 DeSotos for many years. The main drawback to the service taxis is that they do not leave until the car is full—five passengers plus driver, so you cannot count on being where you want at a specific time. You can pay fares for five and have the cab to yourself, though, if you choose.

Only a few years ago, Karnak and service taxis were the only choices for in-country travel. But with Syria opening to the outside world and the country's growing awareness of its historical heritage, tourism is developing. This shows in the increasing number of private buses, some of which operate regular service between cities, as well as group charters. Prices vary but are still relatively inexpensive, and the private buses are newer and more comfortable than the Karnak fleet. Some are even smoke-free.

Finally, Syrian Air flies between most cities, and is also a bargain, in-country. A flight from Damascus to Latakia can be as low as 600 SP, about US$ 12 for a 320-km (200-mile) flight. You should also fly Syrian Air while you're here; it's the service taxi of the air, and an experience you'll never forget. None of the usual regulations about seatbelts, seat backs and smoking are enforced, and you might feel as though you're part of a comedy movie about an airline rather than actually on a real one. Despite this mode of operation, the airline has a good safety record.

LODGING

If you are particular about cleanliness and comfort in your hotels yet do not want to spend a fortune on a room, you will have to adjust your attitude one way or another. Most hotels are either five-star places with some of the highest prices in the world (a minimum of US$ 250 for a double room during the high season from late May to early October) or dirty, noisy places with little or no hot water, uncomfortable beds, inadequate bedding, rock-hard pillows and bath towels the size of large dinner napkins. There are only a few exceptions to these extremes.

The good news is that if you have an *iqaama*, you can stay at the luxury hotels for about a quarter of what a tourist must pay. This still means the equivalent of US$ 80 (but in local currency) at the Cham Hotel in Latakia for a seaside room during peak season. The best deal is to avoid the peak season. Off-season rates for a seaside room then range from 1,200 to 1,800 SP (US$ 24–36). Also, the small, inexpensive hotels in the mountains seem to be cleaner and more comfortable than those in the cities or desert. One more thing to consider is that the cheapest hotels often have no generators, which means no lights, heat or fan for several hours each day if the electricity is off.

REGIONAL TRAVEL

Because of its central location, Syria is a good base for travel to southern and eastern Europe, North Africa, southeastern Africa, central Asia and the Middle East. Flights out of Damascus are not as plentiful as they are from most cities this size, but they are adequate, and flights to any of these places take at most a few hours.

Visas

Whenever you enter Syria, you must complete duplicate information cards, one of which is stamped by customs and given back to you. Do not lose the card, because you must turn it in when you leave the country. If you don't have it, you will be delayed and often charged 100–200 SP. I stapled mine inside my passport because the passport and immigration (P&I, called *hejera wa jwazaat* in Arabic) office lost it a couple of times.

Syria also requires an exit visa: if you are a resident you cannot leave the country without one. The good news is that you can usually get it in a day or two through any P&I office.

You first need a letter from your employer or sponsor in the country, then you go to the P&I office (in Damascus there is one centrally located near the Damascus University Law School and Karnak bus station in the neighbourhood called Baramkeh). Here, at a little office two doors south of the main entrance, you buy a few stamps, go to the third floor and pay 10 SP for an application, complete the application, go to the fourth floor for a signature and return the application with your passport and sponsor's letter to the third floor. If you do this early enough (usually before 10 am), you can sometimes pick it up around 1 pm the same day. At the latest, it should be ready the next day. The office will hold your *iqaama* until you return to the country, so your first task after returning should be to go to the P&I office, show them your passport, and retrieve your *iqaama*.

Customs

My experience with customs officials both entering and leaving has been mostly positive. They seem to allow visitors from the West to enter with a minimum of hassle. But sexually explicit materials will get you in trouble if they're spotted, and illegal drugs will land you in jail. In the mid-1990s, a young American woman served a five-year prison sentence for attempting to bring in drugs.

You must deal with customs not only when you arrive, but any time you leave the country. Border crossings by land are time-consuming, because you must stop for customs in Syria, then again in Turkey, Jordan or Lebanon. The customs agents are mainly interested in the amount of currency you are leaving with (don't tell them you have more than a couple of hundred Syrian pounds or any large amounts of hard currency), illegal drugs or antiquities. In the latter, they most often look for antique carpets and mosaics, so if you have new ones, you may have to do some convincing that the items are not antiques. It helps to have a receipt.

The Middle East

Jordan and Lebanon are closest to Syria. Folks who go to Lebanon do so primarily for the metropolitan amenities of

Beirut, the most European city in the Levant. Jordan's capital Amman is a fairly new city with lovely modern architecture and is spread out over seven hills. Compared to Damascus, it is quite clean and full of open spaces, but because of its relative newness as a metro area, has little of the historical or cultural interest that Damascus offers. Nationwide, however, Jordan does contain many historical sites, the wonder of Petra (an ancient city carved into multicoloured sandstone cliffs), the magnificent Wadi (canyon, in Arabic) Rum with its exotic cliffs and isolation, and the resort of Aqaba on the Red Sea. The mountains of southern Jordan are rugged and exotically beautiful. There are also resorts on the Dead Sea.

Entrance Visas

Both Jordan and Lebanon require entrance visas, but you can get one for Jordan at the border crossing. It costs 10 Jordanian dinars (about US$ 14) for nationals from most countries.

Visiting Israel is also a possibility via Jordan—the only Arab country of the Levant from which you can do so at this time. Since Jordan and Israel have signed a peace agreement, it's quite easy to travel between them. The main border crossings are on the road between Amman and Jerusalem and between the 'twin' cities of Aqaba (Jordan) and Elath (Israel) on the Red Sea. Most Westerners don't need a visa to enter Israel—only a passport.

At any rate, Jordan is the only country of the Levant at this time that will definitely allow you entry if you have an Israeli stamp in your passport. Make sure Israeli customs does not stamp your passport if you want to enter another Arab country again without a hassle or rejection (they can stamp a separate piece of paper that you keep in your passport while in Israel, then toss out before returning to Syria). Once when I was at the border crossing to Turkey, a group of young people had travelled by bus all the way from Istanbul (a very long two-day trip), only to be refused entry to Syria because they had Israeli stamps in their passports.

Going to other Arab countries on the Peninsula is a bit more difficult. You cannot get a tourist visa to Saudi Arabia, and you must be sponsored by someone who lives in the other Gulf countries or by a hotel there. Air fares to and from Gulf countries are also expensive. For example, a round trip flight between Damascus and Dubai costs nearly as much as an off-season ticket between Damascus and New York—about three times as far away.

There are two countries on the Arabian peninsula you can easily get a tourist visa for: Yemen and Oman. Yemen is the ancient land of the queen of Sheba and a fascinating combination of African, south Asian, and Arab cultures and unique architecture. It is also a rugged, mountainous country with cool temperatures in the highlands, despite its proximity to the equator. The Yemenis, like Syrians, are friendly people who are interested in outsiders. Oman is an exotic place with gorgeous landscapes and sea and friendly, multi-cultural people.

North Africa (the Maghreb)

The easiest country in this area to visit is Egypt. A visa is necessary, but you can get one upon arrival at the airport. A flight from Damascus to Cairo takes around two hours, to Luxor or Aswan about an hour longer. There are other routes of entrance to Egypt, as well. One—to the Sinai—is via Aqaba in southern Jordan. You can go to the Egyptian consulate in Aqaba to get a visa, then take a ferry to the southern tip of the Sinai or to the Red Sea coast. The other is a nearly two-day trip via ferry from Latakia to Alexandria.

Other countries of the Maghreb require visas in advance, and these can be obtained at their respective embassies in Damascus. Your choice of airlines to these destinations is limited.

Southeastern Africa

A few expats in Syria travel to places like Kenya, Botswana and other countries of eastern Africa. Flights are relatively expensive, but much cheaper than they would be from just about any place else, and Africa is full of natural wonders.

You can also visit Madagascar and Mauritius easily. It's wise to check into local conditions at your intended destination before taking off, however. Also make sure you have every necessary inoculation.

Central and Southern Asia

People from many Western countries are either forbidden or discouraged by their governments from entering Iran or are not welcomed by the fundamentalist regime. Despite this, and despite Teheran's apparent support of violent Islamic radicals, the country seems to be a safe place to travel. As an American, I wouldn't go there, but an Australian friend who did was treated well and enjoyed his visit. An entrance visa is required.

The former Soviet republics in central Asia are not far away, but transportation to them is limited and the safety of some is questionable at this time because of civil unrest. There are also still few visitors' facilities in most of these countries. If the countries of the region become more stable, they will be interesting places to visit—many of them are complete unknowns to the rest of the world.

Turkey, although mostly in Asia, feels more like Europe than Asia or the Middle East, particularly around the coastal regions. It is a fascinating, huge country, and one that is full of historical and exotic places. Turkish people also tend to be quite friendly and accepting, and even though the percentage of its Muslim population is much greater than that of Syria, the atmosphere is quite different in numerous ways. One place I highly recommend to visit is Cappadocia, a vast area of weathered volcanic ash formations where early groups of people carved houses and churches into the cliffs and even entire underground cities. If you have read Tolkien's *The Hobbit*, you might think this the perfect setting for the story. The 'Turquoise Coast' as the central Turkish Mediterranean coastline is called, is also spectacularly beautiful, with many interesting areas. Turkey is only a few hours by bus or air from Syria, and is far less expensive than most of Europe. And then, of course, there are the world-famous Turkish carpets. My partner and I spent nearly two weeks in Turkey, traveling first by bus from Syria then by the great, convenient Turkish bus system along most of the Turquoise Coast, and the total cost—including two carpets we bought was only about US$ 1,500.

Europe

Greece and Italy are only two to four hours away by plane, Cyprus only an hour's flight or a day-long ferry ride from Latakia. At the farthest reaches of western Europe, the British Isles and Scandinavian countries can be reached in five or six hours.

Eastern Europe, still a travel bargain, although generally with fewer amenities than western Europe, is very close. Sofia (Bulgaria), Bucharest and Budapest are within three hours by air, the Czech and Slovak Republics and Poland an hour or two more. Most countries in eastern Europe still require entrance visas, and these should be obtained before buying your ticket. There should be no trouble getting one, but it could take a while.

GROUP TRAVEL

It seems that at least once a year, someone from an international school or embassy organises a group tour to some part of Turkey, Syria or Jordan. Try to find out about these, because not only do they make travel less expensive, they are a good way to meet other expats. Also, if you do not know the area well you will discover and see things in a tour that you might miss if you go by yourself.

LEARNING THE
LANGUAGE

CHAPTER 8

'Arabs love fine and sonorous words for their own sake,
and care for poetry and rhetoric more than the other arts...
Through language and imagination again there enters an
ethical system which exalts the heroic virtues: loyalty to
friends, family, tribe; the sense of personal and family
honour; hospitality; the magnanimity of the strong
man (sic) who does not always insist on his rights.'
—Albert Hourani, Arab historian

THE ARABIC LANGUAGE IS ANCIENT—its roots go back thousands of years; and because of its holy status in the Koran, it has probably changed less over the last thousand years than any other major language; think of English from the nearly incomprehensible Chaucer to Shakespeare to modern American English, and realise that during a period several hundred years longer than that, standard Arabic (at least in written form) has not changed at all. The differences between Arabic and English are so vast that even native speakers of each who become proficient in the vocabulary and grammar of the other have difficulty with the opposing rhetorical styles. These styles are more than superficial: they are at the heart of the cultural gulf and the often incompatible views of life that divide Arabic- and English-speaking peoples.

Because Arabs have a rich oral tradition, the spoken word is supreme. Raphael Patai, in his book *The Arab Mind*, claims that the oral mastery of even illiterate desert and village Arabs is extraordinary, and that their eloquence in their native language makes the English of the average American seem like a "series of disjointed grunts". This love of and superlative use of language is obvious in that most Arabs—even many who are uneducated—can still function to some extent in foreign languages; and virtually all educated Arabs excel in foreign languages.

DIFFERENCES IN USAGE

The groups that use English as their main language have developed the linguistic and cultural values of understatement (particularly in the British variety), scientific precision, use of logic, and brevity. In other words, say what you mean clearly, using as few words as possible. Groups whose primary language is Arabic, on the other hand, have developed the cultural and linguistic values of overstatement, exaggeration, repetition and emotional appeal.

Emotions

In *The Arab Mind*, the author says: "... no language I know comes even near to Arabic in its power of rhetoricism, in its ability to penetrate beneath and beyond intellectual comprehension directly to the emotions and make its impact upon them. In this respect, Arabic can be compared only to music. For speakers of English, the effect their language has on them is very different from that of great music. Yet the speakers of Arabic react to both language and music in a basically similar manner, except that their reaction to the language is probably deeper, more intense, and more emotional."

Another Arab scholar, Edward Atiyah, claims that Arabs are more swayed by words than by ideas, more by ideas than by facts. While educated native English speakers might be impressed and their thinking influenced by an eloquent, logical argument in English, an Arab—often the educated as well as the illiterate—will most often be impressed and won over by powerful emotional arguments. My own experience of teaching students from all over the world has shown me that this is true; Arabs seem to be very emotional people with language, whether their own or others they learn.

These divergent emotional aspects of the two languages create a communication barrier. While an educated native English speaker usually has little respect for an emotional appeal, branding it as demagoguery or a sign of weak thinking, an Arab feels that the cool, detached, fact-filled arguments of a Westerner mark the person as cold and unfeeling.

Hyperbole and Repetition

The difference in discourse style becomes vividly apparent when trying to teach Arab students how to write in a style suitable for American business and academia. Their verbose and repetitive writing is often overwhelming. I have read multi-page essays that say the same thing over and over, in slightly different ways. As an example, here is an excerpt from a book—written in English—by Dr. M.S.R. Al Booty, an Islamic scholar, entitled *This Is Islam: An Introduction Towards Understanding the Roots: Who Am I? Why? and: Where to?*

"Some of these fascinated Westernised people harked to a few of those Calls and rushed to those Islamic readings, concentrating on these sides—as economics and legislation —which interest them, but—till now—I have not learned that anyone of them admired the branches of Islam, and this admiration led him to the doctrinal roots and origins, and turned, later on, from the ideological admiration of the Islamic system to the mental and heart admiration of the doctrinal Islamic facts."

Some Arabist scholars believe that a subdued or understated response from a native Arabic speaker means

little or no commitment or assertion. So if a native English speaker makes a firm but subdued commitment or assertion, it is perceived by an Arab listener as weak or doubtful. One scholar declared that Arabs are forced by their culture to overstate and exaggerate in all communication or risk being misunderstood.

Overstatement is also used for politeness. If you say *marhaba* or *ahlan* (hello) to a Syrian, the answer will usually be *marhabtain* or *ahlain* (two hellos) or *ahlan wa sahlan* (hello and welcome). In other words, the response must outdo the initial greeting, goodbye, etc.

Words in Lieu of Action

Another characteristic of Arabic that is mostly foreign to English speakers is the use of verbal threats without action, and this may magnify conflicts between Arabs and others. For years, Arab politicians have made threats that they not only could not keep, but had no intention of keeping. This is "sabre rattling" at its finest, but if they talk about doing something, they are unlikely to carry out the action. The problem is, people from a culture where idle threats are not often made perceive the verbal threat as a prelude to action, and act accordingly.

Patai says: "... the verbal statement of a threat or an intention (especially when it is uttered repeatedly and exaggeratedly) achieves such importance that the question of whether or not it is subsequently carried out becomes of minor significance. There is no confusion between words and action, but rather a psychologically conditioned substitution of words for action."

OTHER DIFFERENCES

In addition to the functional differences in Arabic and English, there are significant structural (grammatical) and phonetic (sound) differences.

Time Sense and Verbs

English verbs denote very specific senses of time. With a few specific exceptions, past means past, present continuous means present, and so on. But Arabic verbs, although they are more regular than those in English, are quite hazy about time; the basic forms are the perfect (past) and the imperfect (non-past). In the Koran, Allah is sometimes described as doing something simultaneously in both the past and future, and Mary the mother of Jesus appears to be a contemporary of Mary the sister of Moses in places. Arab historians and biographers, too, have often been hazy about the specific time or duration of an event, according to some scholars.

This apparent disregard for time and chronology shows in day-to-day living among Arab people. In Syria, for example, even such modern operations as bus lines and airlines operate almost as if the stated schedules or times on tickets are not terribly important. Arabs in general seem to worry little about time (or age) and Syrians seem more that way to me than do the Jordanians or Lebanese. Because of modern industries this characteristic seems to be changing a bit among younger people.

Another grammatical curiosity of Arabic vis-à-vis English is that Arabic does not use a present-tense form of the verb 'be', or 'copula', as it is called in linguistics. For example, in English I would say "I am a teacher" or "I am tall." But in Arabic I say *Ana modarress* (a double 'r' is trilled as in Spanish) or *Ana taweel*—literally "I teacher" and "I tall".

Nouns and Adjectives

Nouns in Arabic have either male or female gender, as they do in the Romance languages. This is the easy part. The more difficult things are that: 1) there are verbal nouns, and 2) nouns have three different forms—which sometimes seem unrelated—when used with numbers. There is one form for one and 11 or more of something (*mara*, one woman, for example); another form for two of anything, which is simply the first noun with -ain (masculine) or -tain (feminine) added (*maratain*, two women); and a third form for three to ten of something (*tlaat niswaan*, three women).

Arabic uses no nonspecific articles (a, an), but most common nouns take the specific article 'al', which does not change for gender. Adjectives, however, need gender agreement with the nouns they modify, and the forms of some (such as colours) seem unconnected to each other: *aswad* (masc. black) and *soda* (fem. black), for example. To complicate matters, colours are often the names of food in the Syrian dialect: *aswad* is one word for eggplant, *soda* is a word for liver, and *bayd*, a variation of feminine white, is used for eggs.

Linguistic Sexism

In English, the infinitive is 'to' plus a verb; in Arabic, it is the same form as used for third person 'he' in the past tense: 'he ate, he slept, etc'. Words with associated meanings in Arabic use the same root consonants. One such root is the same for little boy, children in general and giving birth. Also, the word commonly used for son (*ibn*) is different from that used for male child (*walid*), while both daughter and girl child are described by the same word, *bint*. Verb endings, too, are different, depending on whether one is speaking to a male, a female or a group.

The Script

Arabic is written and read from right to left and shares its script with Farsi, the language of Iran. There are no capital letters, but many letters change form considerably depending on where they appear in a word—beginning, middle or end. In addition, there are several different styles of writing in which some letters are shaped quite differently from others.

There are two major difficulties with reading modern standard Arabic without a large vocabulary, even if one knows the script well. One is that the marks indicating short vowels and double consonants are not used. Without these symbols, it's often difficult to know what word you're reading. Imagine, for example, reading English with all short vowel sounds omitted: pen, pin, pan and pun would all be spelled 'pn'! The second difficulty is that word boundaries are difficult to decipher because there are no spaces separating words as there are in English. Thus, without a fairly strong vocabulary knowledge, one doesn't know where one word ends and the next begins.

Pronunciation

Several Arabic sounds have no equivalent in English or most other major languages. This alone makes it more difficult for an English speaker to learn than European languages are. Another difficulty in pronunciation is presented by the consonant clusters that often start words. Examples: *BteHki* (you speak), *bmeshi* (I walk), *zbeeb* (raisins) and *tmaneh* (eight). Each consonant in these clusters is pronounced without a detectable vowel sound between them. Several other Arabic sounds vary slightly from their English counterparts. Finally, there are both single and double consonant sounds and single and double vowel sounds; this means that if one does not hold the sound long enough or too long, a completely different word will be uttered.

SOME USEFUL WORDS AND EXPRESSIONS

The words overleaf are written as they should be pronounced. Some of the words and/or pronunciations are unique to Syria or even Damascus. When two of the same consonants appear together, you must pronounce both: *tammam* is pronounced 'tam-mam', not 'ta-mam' as it would be in English. Also, 'h' sounds (there are two: 'h' represents an English-type sound, while 'H' represents a heavier 'h' sound) are pronounced no matter where they come in a word, except in the 'kh' and 'gh' combinations, which represent individual Arabic letters.

Greetings, Goodbyes, Miscellaneous	
marHaba or ahlan	Hello
sabaH al khair	Good morning (or early afternoon)
sabaH an noor	response to sabaH al khair
masa al khair	Good evening.

Greetings, Goodbyes, Miscellaneous

masa an noor	response to masa al khair
as salaam aleeikom	God's peace be with you (a greeting)
yaiatik alaiafee	A greeting and goodbye to someone who is working; may God keep you able to work
maia salaameh	Goodbye (literally, with peace); to a person leaving
tammam or kwayyis	Good. Fine. I agree.
min faddlak	Please; usually after a request (to a man)
min faddlik	Please; usually after a request (to a woman)
shukran	Thank you.
aiafwan	You are welcome; also "Excuse me."
naiam or eh	Yes
laa	No
biddee	I want …
maa biddee	I don't want …
fee	There is/are.
fee?	Is/Are there?
maa fee	There isn't/aren't.
addaish?	How much?
kem?	How many?
ana assif	I'm sorry (from a man).
ana asfee	I'm sorry (from a woman).
maialish	No problem. It's OK.
hadha	this
Ismee ——	My name is ——.
hown	here
hineek	there

Greetings, Goodbyes, Miscellaneous	
al yassar	left
al yameen	right
dooghree	straight

Days, Time	
Sunday	*al aHid*
Monday	*at tnayn*
Tuesday	*at tlaata*
Wednesday	*al arbaia*
Thursday	*al khamees*
Friday	*al jumaiah*
Saturday	*as sabt*
a day	*yom*
a week	*isbooa*
a month	*shaHr*
a year	*saneh*
today	*al yom*
tonight	*al layla*
yesterday	*mbareh*
tomorrow	*bukra*
a minute	*daeea*
an hour	*saaia*

Numbers	
zero	*sufr*
one	*waHd*
two	*itnayn*
three	*tlaateh*
four	*arbaia*
five	*khamseh*
six	*sitteh*
seven	*sabaia*

Numbers	
eight	*tmaneh*
nine	*tisaia*
ten	*aiashara*

Common Signs & Words	
Exit	*Mah-raj*
Entrance, for car	*Mad-ha-loos'say-ar-rot*
pedestrian	*Mad-ha-loo-l'sot*
Open	*Maf-too*
Closed	*Moog-lak*
Toilet	*Mir-had or Too- wah-let*
Toilet paper	*Wrah-lak too-wa-let*
Woman	*Mah-rah*
Man	*Rah-jool*
Customs	*Joom-ruk*
passport	*ja-wahs'sfar*
visa	*tah-see-rah*
Bus	*Bas*
Taxi	*Taxi*
Train	*Kee-tar*

Stores and Businesses	
bakery	*mah-bajz*
bank	*mahs-reef*
bookstore	*mak-tah-bah*
grocery	*doo-kah-noo l'bak-kal*
jeweler	*jah-ha-ree*
market	*sook (souq)*
news stand	*koos-koo l'jah-rah-eed*
pharmacy	*sigh-dah-lee-yah*

Stores and Businesses	
post office	*mak-tab bah-reed*
restaurant	*mah-tam*
shoemaker	*al-hadd-dah*
supermarket	*supermarket*
travel agency	*mak-tah-boo s'see-ya-ha*
credit card	*bit-ah-kah-too lee-still-aff*
traveler's check	*seek see-yah-hee*
price/rate	*seer*
fax	*te-le-fax*
letter	*ree-sah-la*
stamp	*tah-bee-yoo l' bar-eed*
postcard	*bit-ak-kah bar-eed-ah*

Food	
bread	*khubz*
flour	*taHeen*
milk	*Haleeb*

Accommodation Terms	
hotel	*foon-dook*
balcony	*ball-kon*
bathroom	*ham-mam*
bathtub	*bon-yoh*
blanket	*bah-tahn-nee-yah*
breakfast	*foo-toor*
camping	*tah-yeem*
to clean	*naz-za-fa*
change of linen	*tab-dee-loo l'bah-yah-dat*
dinner	*ah-sah*
fan	*meer-wah-ha-too t'tah-wee-yah*

BODY LANGUAGE

When Syrians talk to each other, they stand close and use lots of hand gestures, much like the stereotype of Italians. They tend to speak loudly as well. Such characteristics are likely to make a newcomer think a fight is imminent, but this is not the case. Even what in the West would be considered an aggressive stance—standing close and leaning toward another person—is normal and not an indication of aggressive behaviour there.

There are several head movements that a visitor to Syria should understand. A quick upward movement of the head with raised eyebrows, often accompanied by closed eyelids and a click of the tongue means 'no'. A downward nod to one side means 'yes'. A movement of the head from side to side, often accompanied by a puzzled look, means 'I don't understand' or 'I didn't hear you'. If you wag your head from side to side to say no or move the head up, raising the eyebrows slightly to mean something like 'I'm sorry, I didn't catch what you said', you are likely to be misunderstood.

Hand gestures here are similar to those in some other countries around the eastern Mediterranean.

- A common gesture is the palm turned upward, the fingertips together forming a tent over the palm; the hand and forearm pumps up and down, arm flexing at the elbow. The listener is asked to wait until the speaker is finished.
- Another is palms up and open, arms out to the side and raised as if to catch raindrops. This is the 'What's going on here?' pose that's used a lot in traffic.
- Opened hands drawn quickly above the shoulders, palms facing the other person sends this message 'That's my point' or 'That's my excuse'.
- Brushing the open palms together quickly as if to clean off dirt means 'I'm finished with it (you)' or 'I wash my hands of it (you)'.
- If you're in a crowd at a vegetable stand and the shopkeeper looks at you, gives a quick sideways wag

of his head and pivots his hand, palm up at about chest
level, he's asking what you would like.

- Another common gesture is touching the right hand to
  the heart and sometimes to the forehead when meeting
  friends by chance. This shows affection and fondness
  for the person. Using this gesture while saying No
  (turning down an invitation, for example) somewhat
  softens the blow of rejection.

ARABIC DIALECTS AND OTHER LANGUAGES

Although standard written Arabic (both the classic and
modern forms) is the same throughout the Middle East,
colloquial dialects are far more diverse than are worldwide
English dialects; so much so, in fact, that a Damascene
has trouble understanding an Egyptian, and an Omani
and Moroccan can understand very little of each other's
spoken language.

Dialects

The dialectical differences are not only in pronunciation
and intonation—great as these often are—but in the use of
different words. An older Syrian woman told me that when
she visited Morocco and went to a vegetable souk, nearly
every item had a name different from that used in Syria. Also,
the Egyptian dialect is notorious for using a lot of words that
are different from other dialects.

Even from city to city within Syria, there are noticeable
variations, and the greater the distance, the greater the
difference. I could communicate fairly well in Amman,
Jordan, about 320 km (200 miles) from Damascus, but
in Aqaba (on the Red Sea) I can barely do so. If you only
learn the Damascene dialect you will have some trouble
communicating in Deir er-Zor (on the Euphrates River). In
fact, a report in http://www.ethnologue.com lists no less than
SIX major Arabic dialects within Syria. This is complicated by
the fact that there are at least nine other ancient languages
still spoken by small groups within the country.

Other Languages

The most popular and widely spoken foreign language in Syria is English, with French perhaps a close second. After English and French is German, then Russian. Most educated people speak at least a little of one of these—students in high school are required to study either English or French for a couple of years, and a fair number can converse in several different languages.

If you stay in Damascus and work around English speakers, you can generally get by with only a survival level of Arabic. But other cities seem to have fewer English speakers, and rural areas and villages have few people who speak anything but their own dialect of Arabic. To put it another way, this is not Europe, where most educated people speak several languages. Taxi drivers, bus drivers and clerks in government offices rarely speak anything but Arabic, and the residue of French occupation shows in government forms and signs that are often printed in both Arabic and French.

Another communication problem for visitors is that most natives who speak English do not speak it very well. The differences between Arabic and English discussed earlier in this chapter account for some odd usages of words and grammar as well as pronunciations that are often difficult to understand. Most Syrians I know who speak English as clearly as, say, the average educated German, are those who either learned it in childhood or have lived for several years in an English-speaking country.

Other ancient languages are still alive in Syria. In Maalula and the surrounding area (an hour's drive north of Damascus) Aramaic—the language of Christ—is still spoken. In the far northwestern corner of the country the Armenian language is so common that signs are in both Arabic and Armenian and Armenian children learn their ancestral language along with Arabic. There are a few speakers of Syriac (one of the original languages of Syria) and of Kurdish in the northeastern part of the country. Some Jews can speak or at least read Hebrew.

Learning Arabic

If you want to study Arabic, you have numerous options.

Arabic Language Center (ALC) of The Language Institute at Damascus University

Established in 1995 (Arabic), 2002 for 12 other languages; very well-equipped and uses modern teaching techniques. Cost around US$ 300 per month.

Contact: Rahaj Ajouka

Office of Registration & Students' Affairs

Damascus University

Mezzeh Highway Fayez Mansour St.—Campus of Humanities

Phone: 392-5843 (In Damascus)

Fax: 212-0164 (In Damascus)

Email: inquiries@arabicindamascus.edu.sy

Arabic Teaching Institute for Foreigners in Mezzeh

Two sessions annually with four levels, each about six months in duration, that cost US$ 400 at this time, books not included. Classes tend to be quite a bit larger than those at the ALC. Classes meet 3.5 hours daily (afternoons only), five days each week (no Friday or Sunday classes). All students, from beginners through advanced, are taught in standard Arabic— a problem, obviously, if you speak and understand none. In addition to the regular classes, there are conversation and newspaper reading classes.

Contact:

Dr Hazem Alwani

PO Box 9340,

Mezzeh-Villat Sharkiyah

Damascus, Syria

Phone: 613-2646 (In Damascus)

Private Classes

This option most used by foreigners, it seems, is a private tutor. Many Syrians will give you private lessons for prices ranging from about 250–750 SP per hour. Check around with expats who have had experience with tutors to find a good one, or visit the following websites: http://www.tolearnarabic.com/learnarabic/aboutus.html or http://www.arabekstudiesindamascus.com.

Damascus Community School

This is an option for children at a K–12 school sponsored by the US State Department. One of the Syrian teachers here usually offers Arabic lessons at various levels during the autumn term. Located in the Abu Romaneh area. Telephone: 333-7737 (In Damascus)

Two other options—if you are fairly fluent in French or German—are at the French Cultural Centre and the German Goethe Centre. Whichever way you choose to learn the language, you will have a lot of opportunity to practice. Syrians appreciate your attempts to communicate in their language and will help you all they can.

DOING BUSINESS
IN SYRIA

CHAPTER 9

'In the transnational economy the goal is not
profit maximisation. It is market maximisation.
And trade increasingly follows investment.'
—Peter F. Drucker, *The New Realities*

ECONOMIC AND RELATED SITUATIONS

The United States Embassy commercial section classifies Syria as a "middle income developing country". Although poverty exists there and only a few people are wealthy, the number of middle- and upper-class people has grown quite noticeably since the early 1990s, and signs of wealth are continually increasing. Real economic growth rates are a bit tricky to pin down, as the Syrian versions differ a lot from those of the World Bank, the IMF and European and North American estimates, but as the effects of the global financial crisis were felt in Syria, the country's growth rate slowed to 1.8 per cent in 2009. Exports increased from about US$ 2.5 billion in 2005 to around US$ 14 billion in 2008, only to go down to US$ 10 billion in 2009. However, manufacturing, banking, tourism and other private industries funded by both foreign and Syrian sources are increasing, especially for basic products such as medicines, clothing and household goods.

As I mentioned earlier, Syria has been under a socialist system since its independence. Until recently, only small farms and shops were private operations. The state-run industries have had to import heavy equipment and raw materials, but except for necessities, there were few imported goods and no foreign business operations. From the 1960s until the disintegration of the Soviet Union, most imports (except cars) came from the USSR under a bilateral trade agreement it had with Syria.

This has changed, opening possibilities for new imports, joint ventures, and construction projects. Investment law #10, put into effect in early 1991 and amended in 2000 to further open the country for private investment, liberalises some currency restrictions, gives tax holidays of 5–7 years and other incentives for certain private investment.

The Negatives

The Syrian government and Chambers of Commerce as well as some industrial and commercial sectors are trying hard to lure foreign investments and in doing so paint a rather rosy picture of how great the business and social environment are becoming in Syria. And while it's true that many new laws, rules and directives have made the situation for foreign (as well as Syrian) investors better, there's still a long way to go in creating a system in which things operate openly and as they are supposed to. So first, let me start with some of the negative factors.

Abu Shady, last of the traditional Syrian storytellers. He performs at the Al Nawfara Cafe in Damascus' old city, telling stories from ages past.

The Western Gate of Souq Al-Hamidiyya, the largest souq in Syria. It is located in Damascus, next to the Citadel.

The Citadel which stands at the centre of the old city of Aleppo in Northern Syria. This castle is considered one of the oldest and largest of its kind in the world.

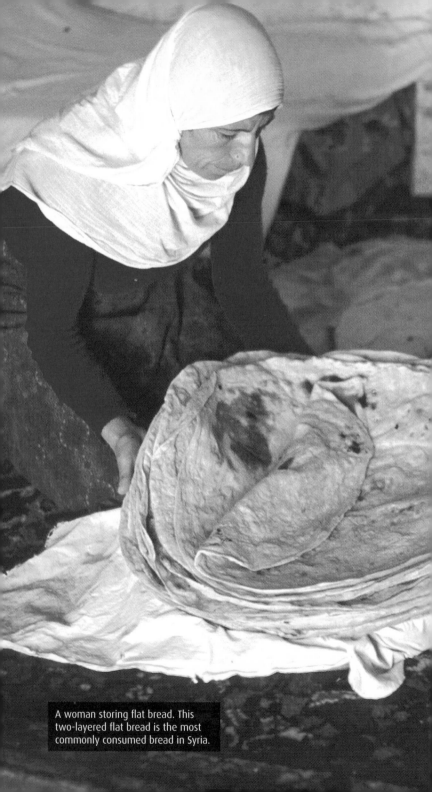

A woman storing flat bread. This two-layered flat bread is the most commonly consumed bread in Syria.

The International Trade Center of the UN Comtrade division conducted a survey of numerous businesses operating in Syria to determine what most saw as the main problems in doing business there. Fourteen factors were listed and respondents were asked to choose the five most problematic. The rankings are as follows, in descending order of importance:

- Inefficient government bureaucracy
- Access to financing
- Corruption
- Inadequately educated work force
- Foreign currency regulations

These five were followed closely by:

- Inadequate infrastructure
- Restrictive labour regulations
- Tax regulations
- Poor work ethic in national work force

In addition to these, the commercial section of the British Embassy notes the following problems (with the caveat that the situation, in most cases, is improving): problems getting bid and performance bonds returned upon completion of a project; governments having a poor record of payment; and import duties being high, creating a problem for profitable sales of manufactured products.

For US-based companies or individuals, the situation has added problems, namely, that the US government discourages doing business in Syria. In addition to listing Syria as a country that supports terrorism and the Central Bank of Syria (CBS) as a money-laundering institution, in 2003, President Bush and the then right-wing Congress created the Syrian Accountability and Lebanese Sovereignty Act (SAA), which severely restricts products that can be exported to Syria and requires case-by-case licensing for most. (In 2005, there were 277 license applications from American businesses, of which only 173 were approved.) US banks have also severed connections with the CBS, making it very difficult for American businesses or individuals using bank accounts in the US to transfer funds between the two countries. In fact, all the US-based oil companies appear to have withdrawn from Syria, and the US embassy commercial section openly states that it does not encourage investments or doing business with or in Syria.

The Positives

The aforementioned problems aside, however, most government and commercial sectors do sincerely want to develop an effective climate for business.

The UN's View

In June 2005, Syria... adopted the Tenth Five Year Plan 2006–2010. This plan highlights the greater expected role of the Syrian private sector in both economic activity and decision-making.

Decision makers are aware of the new requirements of open market economy and the need for competitive business environment... as well as investment-friendly legislation and administrative frameworks. As a result, more than half of the 80 laws and 80 legislative decrees issued in 2005 and 2006 have been targetted toward modernising and promoting the business environment.... Other big steps were taken with respect to modernising the physical and technical infrastructure (ports, the increasing number of customs clearances and modern industrial cities) and increase in budget allocated for higher education and health sector.

— *From Dimashikiyyah, N. 'Increasing the Role of the Private Sector'. UNDP Business Development Programme, Damascus.*

Also, despite remaining obstacles to an efficient and effective business climate, an increasing number of countries and their business/industrial sectors appear to be successful in Syria. Countries of the EU have increasing presence; France has a bilateral trade agreement with Syria; the UK, in a joint venture with Syria, is developing a US$ 337 million tourist project on the coast at Tartus; Japan and Russia have increasing presence and investments in the country; Syria has a free trade agreement with other Arab countries and is working toward one with Turkey; and Iran is building Syria's first car manufacturing plant and making a multitude of other investments in the country as well.

Banking, too, has changed considerably with 10 new private banks licensed, most of which can handle letters of credit, currency exchanges and transfers, etc.

Getting Started

The key sectors for investment as of 2007 appear to be oil and gas exploration and tourism, although any projects that hire Syrian workers and use Syrian raw materials are encouraged. Also, in most cases, joint ventures with the government or Syrian businesses are desired, and a recent change in the joint venture ownership law changed the requirement for joint ventures to be owned at least 51 per cent by Syria, allowing majority ownership (51 per cent) by outside investors. The country has also established seven free zones in which investments are particularly liberalised and encouraged. These are: Damascus; Adra (25 km north of Damascus); Damascus International Airport (now fully occupied, but to be expanded); Allepo, Syria's second-largest city; Tartus (on the coast, near Lebanon); Latakia (on the coast in the north); and Dera'a (on the border with Jordan).

If you decide you want to start a business or extend your existing business to Syria, these are the registration requirements for a private incorporated company in Damascus (from the World Bank):

- Step 1.Get forms for articles of incorporation from the Ministry of Economy and Trade. Cost: 250 SP; Time to complete: about a day
- Step 2. Deposit initial capital (minimum of 3 million SP —about US$ 60,000) in bank and get a statement. No charge; about a day
- Step 3. Apply for commercial registration with the Ministry of Economy and Trade. No charge; about 14 days
- Step 4. Submit the company's bylaws to the Court of First Instance; have company's books stamped. No charge; about a day
- Step 5. Pay the stamp tax at the tax office. 0.5 per cent of capital; about a day
- Step 6. Open a financial record for the company at the Tax and Financial Department of the government. No charge; about a day
- Step 7. Make payment to Syrian bar association. 10,500 SP; about a day

- Step 8. Return to court to complete incorporation. 104 SP; about a day
- Step 9. Visit Commercial Registry office with signed copies of articles of incorporation; 50 SP; about 1 day
- Step 10. Register for taxes; no charge; about 14 days
- Step 11. Register with Social Security Organisation. 20 SP; about a day
- Step 12. Have a company seal made; 500 SP; about three days

And, of course, in addition to those requirements, you must hire an attorney for your own protection and assistance with the myriad local laws and procedures. The wisest thing to do would be to contact the commercial section of your own country's embassy and have them assist you throughout the process, get recommendations for local attorneys, etc.

The preceding is for setting up a business in Syria. However, the way many Western companies operate in Syria is via a registered Syrian agent. The agent should be registered with the Companies Department of the Ministry of Economy and Foreign Trade.

Licensing is another way for companies to do business in Syria but without having to cope with all the difficulties of actually operating a business within the country. For example, Canada Dry soft drinks are popular there but are not bottled or sold by the company or its subsidiaries: it is done by a Syrian company under licence to Canada Dry. Another example is a company in Aleppo that manufactures medicines under licence to the French pharmaceuticals company Rhone-Poulenc Rorer. In these licensing arrangements, the outside companies receive royalties for the use of their brand names, expertise, research and recipes. But poor or irregular quality control is a potential problem.

Although potential enterprises are unlimited in principle, businesses are more likely to be approved if they:
- maximise the use of local resources
- create local jobs
- boost Syrian exports

- utilise advanced technologies, and
- assist the government in achieving its development plans

The government prefers joint ventures, which receive 5-7 year tax holidays. The number of local employees and managers are negotiated at the time of licensing. The Ministry of Supply has the authority to set prices and profit margins for products sold locally.

Law No 10 allows foreign enterprises the same tax and foreign exchange benefits as the locals. Additionally, it allows foreigners to repatriate capital after five years (or six months, if the project fails due to something beyond the investor's control—a nebulous qualification) and to transfer hard currency profits annually. Also, foreign employees are allowed to repatriate 50 per cent of their earnings and 100 per cent of any severance pay they receive.

Land ownership laws are complex, and only Syrians are allowed to own real estate. However, no expropriation of private business has occurred since the 1960s, and new investment laws contain strong protection against government seizure.

Property, contractual rights and intellectual property rights are protected by the country's constitution, and the government accepts international arbitration of investment disputes between foreign investors and the state if the investment agreement includes such stipulation; if it does not, local courts have jurisdiction. Syria is a member of the Paris Union for the International Protection of Industrial Property. Patents are issued for 15 years, trademarks for 10 years. The reality is, though, that numerous rip-offs of copyrights and trademarks exist, mostly in the forms of pirated audio/video cassettes, CDs and DVDs, as well as computer software. Nearly all Syrian home videos/DVDs are bootleg copies, as are nearly all music tapes/CDs and a great deal of computer software. At various times, the government has raided computer shops and confiscated pirated programs, but after the heat dies down, they are still available. In 2002, Syria signed onto 1967 Stockholm Convention on Intellectual Property Rights and in 2004 became a member of the World Intellectual Property

Organisation. However, despite occasional crackdowns on violations in these areas, abuse is still rampant.

There are no private trade unions in Syria, but most workers belong to one of the official government unions, organised under the General Federation of Trade Unions (GFTU). In the private sector, this organisation monitors compliance with laws relating to employees' health, safety and pay. There are minimum wage and minimum age laws. Currently, the absolute minimum age is 12, with parental permission required for children under 16 to work. Children are not allowed to work at night.

Standard working hours for office staff who do not serve customers directly are often from 8 or 9 am until 2, 4 or 5 pm. Most businesses are open to the public from 8, 9 or 10 am (depending on the type of business) until around 2 pm. They open again around 4–5 pm and remain open until 8, 9, 10 or even 11 pm.

SOCIAL ASPECTS OF DOING BUSINESS

As with ordinary socialising, there are few taboos in doing business with Syrians. The difficulty some Westerners (particularly North Americans) might have will more likely be caused by the 'all business' demeanour that is often admired in the hard-driving business person in the West. In this part of the world, such a person seems somehow cold-hearted, and if you are perceived that way, you may have difficulty getting a Syrian's business.

Having the best price or best merchandise when trying to make a sale does not matter as much as the personal relationship you develop. Remember, in this culture, your contacts are everything. Before you try doing the hard sell on a Syrian, get to know the person, eat and drink tea together and talk about your families.

Decisions are made slowly here, and if your negotiations fall on the cusp of a holiday (particularly Eid), you will not get a decision until well after the holiday is over. This is often true even if you are the buyer. Most Syrians won't bend over backwards to get your business, regardless of how much you are in a hurry. Here are some other specifics to note.

Greetings

Business greetings are generally a little less ebullient than personal greetings, although the manner will depend on how well the people know each other. As a rule, the handshake has pretty much replaced more affectionate hellos and goodbyes. Handshakes here are quite limp by American standards, with no hand pumping; big grins that expose your rear molars should also be restrained since Syrians don't smile a lot (laugh, yes, but there is a difference).

If you are a man and get to know a male business associate, he may or may not hug you and blow a kiss by both cheeks upon greeting. If he does not, you might endear yourself to him by initiating the action: it will make him feel like you are kin.

If you are a woman dealing with a female business associate, all your hellos and goodbyes will likely be a hug and kisses on both cheeks, possibly starting with your first meeting. Business associates of opposite genders will not hug but will almost always shake (momentarily hold would be a more apt description) hands. If you are a man dealing with a scarved woman, however, you may want to let her take the lead just in case her beliefs will not allow her to touch a man who is not her relative.

Meetings

Syria has no corporate climate as do Western countries. Until only a few years ago, any business larger than a small family operation was owned and operated by government ministries. Endless political and hierarchical meetings were the rule, with narcoleptic people sitting and appearing to listen to a leader talk about the glories of the Party and the country's leadership and how much they—the ministry or company— were doing for the Syrian people.

Group meetings are not as common as in the West, and when they are held, they are generally not democratic, consensus-building meetings, but are conducted by some-one who is unquestionably 'in charge'. This is a strong characteristic of Arab culture, whether in the Persian Gulf, the Levant or North Africa. Even if leaders are not respected or are hated, they will be shown respect by their subordinates.

Appointments

Suppose you have an appointment with a Syrian business person to either buy or sell or just explore the possibilities. Promptness is not important. You may rush around in a panic, thinking you are going to be late, only to arrive 10 minutes late and find your contact person either not there yet or also just arriving. Part of this attribute is cultural, but it is logistical as well: city traffic sometimes crawls and catching a cab or bus can take time.

If you show irritation at a Syrian's keeping you waiting, it will not advance your cause. It is also common for appointments to cancel on you, at the last minute and more than once. Some of these time-related characteristics are beginning to change, but cultural change takes time and Syrians will, I hope, never be like Americans or Japanese in their slavery to the clock.

Dealing with Local Staff

The Party-backed labour unions and government regulations favour the worker over the employer. Punctuality is likely to be a problem but could be overcome by incentives. You'll have trouble firing a Syrian worker simply because he or she is always late to work, does poor quality work or is absent from work a lot. There must be serious grounds for dismissal, such as blatant dishonesty or criminal activity.

Another point worth remembering is that Syrians are not accustomed to democracy in any form. If you are the manager who likes to lead by consensus, your wanting to include your employees in the decision-making process may be perceived by them as a lack of knowledge, leadership or control on your part. This is not to say that you cannot train them in this way and make them feel like an integral part of the business, but move slowly and let them know that you are the leader and expect them to follow—even if a decision was made by committee. There is a certain 'law of the desert' at work here, however subconscious it might be, that will rush in to fill a perceived power vacuum: strong leaders are feared and/or respected, while weak ones will be deposed or taken advantage of.

Manner of Dress

Except for politicians and owners of a few large businesses, business dress in Syria is decidedly casual. Even rich house rental agents and men who own tourist businesses usually wear slacks and only slightly dressy shirts. During hot weather, office dress ranges from blue jeans and T-shirts to slacks and dress shirts for men and from scarf and raincoat to glitzy blouses, skirts and lots of jewellery and make-up for women. When the temperature drops, both genders often wear sweaters and/or outer jackets—even leather coats. The main exceptions I've noticed are five-star hotel employees and some tour guides, who often wear uniforms or blazers.

Payments Due

While some Syrians pay what they owe promptly, it is common for most to take a long time to pay. In cases like this, you must be persistent or you are not likely to get paid at all. A fellow teacher there did some graphic design consulting work for a new business forms company and was not paid for about two months; the owner just kept apologising but said he did not have enough money yet. I helped a former student and his partner complete a dealer application packet from Chrysler Corporation. The agreement was that they would call me back when they had all the information completed and a final letter for me to proof. But they never called, and when I called my student a month or so later I got a nervous response about not being quite ready yet—obviously a lie. I waited for another month and called him again, telling him they could take whatever time they wanted as long as they paid me for the time I had already given them. He did pay me and was terribly apologetic about it, but I am sure he would do the same thing again—he admitted the last time I called him that they had not only sent the application off but had been rejected!

It is just culturally acceptable to take a long time to pay your debts, and I have found that requiring payment in advance is the best solution to the problem. This payment problem holds true for both the private and public sectors, and is often worse in the public sectors because of massive bureaucracy.

Baksheesh

This is a word that to Arabs means tip, but those tips could be either tips or out-and-out bribery, based on Western definitions. If you represent a Western company that does not allow you to 'buy' business, you may have trouble competing against others who have no compunction about doing so. Personal relationships can mean a great deal here, but if a lot of money is at stake and—more importantly—a government ministry or agency is involved, greasing the right person's palm may be a prerequisite to doing business. Do not be too eager, however, to offer such a thing; you may encounter people who will be offended by your suggestion.

'We can have facts without thinking but we
cannot have thinking without facts.'
—John Dewey

Official Name
Syrian Arab Republic (*Al Jumhuriyah al Arabiyah as Suriyah* in Romanised Arabic); Syria for short

Capital
Damascus

National Anthem
Guardians of the Homeland (*Homat el Diyar* in Romanised Arabic). It can be heard at http://www.nationalanthems.info/sy.htm

Time (timezone)
UTC + 2; 7 hours ahead of New York City; daylight savings time early April to late October.

Telephone country code
963

Land
Syria borders Turkey on the north, Iraq on the east, Jordan on the south, Israel, Lebanon and Mediterranean Sea on the west (145 km/90 miles of coastline, not counting the Hattey Peninsula, now under control of Turkey). It is shaped like an irregular triangle; mostly semi-arid and desert plateau with a narrow coastal plain and two ranges of mountains in the west.

Arable land: 24.8 per cent
Irrigated land: 13,300 sq km

Area
Land: 185,180 sq km (71,500 sq miles). Including the Golan
Heights; just a bit larger than the US state of North Dakota
Water: 1,550 sq km (598 sq miles)

Highest point
Mount Hermon—2,814 m (9,232 feet)

Lowest point
Near Lake Tiberias—200 m (656 feet) below sea level

Major rivers and lakes
Rivers: Euphrates, al Balikh, al Khabur, Barada, Orontes
Lakes: Arram, Mzerib (natural); al Assad (formed by dam)

Climate
Desert and steppe: hot, dry, sunny summers (June to August)
and chilly, rainy winters (December to February); temperature
ranges from below freezing in winter to over 40°C (104°F)
in summer; dust storms and sand storms common.

Coast and mountains: warm somewhat humid summers
and cold weather with rain, snow or sleet in winter;
temperature ranges from around 10°C (50°F) in winter to a
little over 30°C (86°F) in summer.

Natural resources
Hydropower, petroleum, phosphates, chrome and manganese
ores, asphalt, iron ore, rock salt, marble, gypsum

Population
22 million (2010 est.)
Life expectancy: Male, 72, Female, 76

Literacy:
Female, 73 per cent; Male, 86 per cent (2004 est.)

Ethnic groups
Arab, 90.3 per cent; Kurds, Armenians and other, 9.7 per cent

Religions
Muslim, 90 per cent (Sunni 74 per cent; other 16 per cent)
Christian, 10 per cent
Jewish, relative handful, mostly in Aleppo

Language and dialects
Six dialects of Arabic, plus nine other languages, including
Kurdish, Armenian, Aramaic and Circassian. Basic English
and French are widely understood in cities.

Government
Nominal republic with authoritarian regime; military and
secret police strong

Administrative divisions
14 provinces (called governorates) which are subdivided into
60 districts (further divided into sub-districts), plus dozens
of cities, towns and villages

Currency
Syrian pounds (SP), also called lira; 2010 US$ exchange rate,
roughly 47 lira per US$

Gross Domestic Product (GDP)
US$ 100.7 billion (2009 estimate)

Agricultural products
Produce: wheat, barley, cotton, lentils, chickpeas, olives,
sugar beets
Meat/dairy: beef, mutton, eggs, poultry, milk

Industries
Petroleum, textiles, food processing, beverages, tobacco,
phosphate rock mining, cement and oil seeds crushing, car
assembly

Exports
Products: crude oil, minerals, petroleum products, fruits and vegetables, cotton fiber, textiles, clothing, meat and live animals, wheat
Amount: US$ 13 billion (2009 est.)
Main partners: Iraq, Germany, Lebanon, Italy, France, Egypt, Saudi Arabia (2008 data)

Imports
Products: machinery and transport equipment, electric power machinery, food and livestock, metal and metal products, chemicals and chemical products, plastics, yarn, paper
Amount: US$ 13.1 billion (2009 est.)
Main sources: Saudi Arabia, China, Russia, Italy, Egypt, UAE, Turkey, Iran (2008 data)

Ports and harbours
Banyas, Latakia

Airports
With paved runways: 29; Without: 75
International: 1
Heliports: 7

Railways
One main system with 2,052 km (1,275 miles) of track

FAMOUS PEOPLE
- Ibrahim Hanano: leader of revolution against French occupation
- Michel Aflaq: co-founder of Pan-Arab Ba'ath Party
- Salah al Din al Bitar: co-founder of Pan-Arab Ba'ath Party
- Hafez al-Assad: could be called the 'father' of modern Syria; one of longest-ruling leaders in the modern world
- Farouk al Sharaa: diplomat and Foreign Minister from 1984; currently Vice-President; highly respected for his diplomacy
- Carlos Menem: the 50th president of Argentina, born to Syrian immigrants in Argentina

- Asalah Mostafa Nasri—currently popular female singer
- Duria Lahham—Syrian actor famous and popular throughout Arab world
- George Wassouf—long-time popular singer in Syria and Lebanon
- Sabah Fakhri—long-time popular singer from Aleppo
- Zakaria Tamer—famous writer of Arabic-language short stories and children's stories

Places of Interest

Too numerous to mention in this space; refer to the chapters on settling in and travel as well as any good travel guidebooks.

CULTURAL QUIZ

It is, of course, not possible to prepare a person for every social situation in an unfamiliar country where actions and reactions may differ dramatically from those to which the visitor is accustomed. Flexibility and cultural awareness is always necessary. This quiz is designed to help readers only in the more common situations they might encounter.

SITUATION 1
You are walking on a crowded sidewalk or in a crowded souk and children push up against you, old women bump into you, and someone gets out of a car, bumping you with the car door. You should:

A yell at the people so they can hear you above the din.
B adjust your attitude and accept the jostling as something you can't change.
C stay away from crowded places in future.
D just show your displeasure with a "dirty" look.

The Best Choice
Response **A** will do no good at all; few Syrians speak your language, and they are accustomed to yelling and talking loudly in public. Response **D** will also be lost on them, since the manner in which you look at someone has little social significance. **C** is only possible if you have a servant who can do all your shopping for you since souks and streets are crowded whenever shops are open. Physical closeness and lack of personal space are part of Arab culture, so **B** is the only viable solution; after a while you'll barely notice it.

SITUATION 2
You are travelling in Syria and see a group of women in colourful clothes walking alongside the road, each with a bundle or container balanced on her head. You think this is a great photo opportunity. You should:

Ⓐ stop the car quickly, jump out and snap a picture before they look away.

Ⓑ drive stealthily up behind them and get a shot when they turn around.

Ⓒ forget it.

Ⓓ ask if you can take their photo.

The Best Choice

Choices Ⓐ and Ⓑ are bad. Most traditional Muslims are averse to photographing women, and if you try to be sneaky you might offend them. Ⓒ is a realistic choice (particularly if you're a man), but you might later wish you had the snapshot. The best action is Ⓓ; if a woman asks their permission, some may indicate "No," but others may not mind. It is not necessary to speak to do this—all you need to do is point to your camera and ask your question with your face.

SITUATION 3

You are sitting in your office with your feet on your desk, talking to a Western co-worker. A Syrian co-worker walks in to talk to you. You should:

Ⓐ acknowledge him or her, get the new conversation over with, and continue with your Western co-worker.

Ⓑ wave with your feet, then talk to the person.

Ⓒ ignore the Syrian and continue your first conversation until it's finished.

Ⓓ take your feet off the desk and acknowledge the co-worker who has just entered.

The Best Choice

The only one of these that is completely unacceptable is Ⓑ. The bottoms of shoes represent filth to Syrians, and to wave with your shoes or in other ways that draw attention to your soles would be a sort of mockery. You could do Ⓐ or Ⓒ, but both would show some disrespect (or cultural ignorance) because of your feet. The most acceptable choice is Ⓓ.

SITUATION 4

You're a Western man with a female Syrian co-worker or student. She's vivacious and wears lots of make-up, jewellery and tight clothes. She's also very friendly to you, stands close when she talks to you (which is often), and you know she's affectionate because she's always hugging and kissing her female friends and walking with them arm-in-arm. All this makes you think she's attracted to you, and you decide to:

Ⓐ ask her to go to dinner with you.

Ⓑ tell her you like her and ask her if she wants to talk about the two of you.

Ⓒ reach out and grasp her hand or arm when she's talking to you.

Ⓓ ask one of her friends if the young woman is interested in you.

The Best Choice

Sorry. There is no best choice here, but **Ⓐ** and **Ⓒ** are the worst. **Ⓒ** might get you in trouble in any number of ways (and scare her as well), and **Ⓐ** wouldn't be allowed by her

family. Her affectionate behaviour with her female friends is no indication at all that she'll do the same with you. **❶** would create gossip and speculation that would overwhelm you in no time.

If you are genuinely interested in the woman and know her fairly well, **❷** is probably all right. If her appearance is as described here, she's certainly not a conservative Muslim so she might be receptive if she really does like you. But be careful; many Syrians dream of Western passports whenever they see a Westerner who's a potential mate. You might be a real 'catch' for her and her family.

Unless you are interested in possible marriage to the woman, just accept her friendliness but push no further. This is not a dating culture, and young people (even in their 20s) are usually not even allowed to be alone with a girlfriend or boyfriend until they're engaged. If you do get involved with a Syrian woman and take away her virginity, you may ruin her chances of getting married. If she gets pregnant by you, you could be in real trouble.

SITUATION 5

You're a woman with a male Syrian student or co-worker who pays a lot of attention to you. He asks personal questions and eventually invites you to his home. You should:

❶ say you'd love to and arrange a time.

❷ say you'd like to but that your fiancee wouldn't like it (whether or not you have one).

❸ ask him what the occasion is and whether there will be other guests; if so, whom?

❹ apologise, but tell him you don't know him well enough yet.

The Best Choice

The best response depends on what you want. Choice **❶** would be a mistake. I don't like to make sweeping generalisations, but to most Syrian men, **❶** would imply that you're either attracted to him romantically or one of those 'loose' Western women they see all the time in the movies there—one date, and you're in bed with a man. Even if the man is fairly enlightened and knowledgeable, he's still likely to wonder about your 'morals' if you eagerly accept. If you would like to go and are interested in him romantically, **❻** is possible if for no other reason than it lets him know you're uncomfortable about the social acceptability of such an invitation. **❹** would be realistic if you do like him—again, this isn't a dating culture. If you don't want to go and want to avoid further invitations and unwelcome pursuit, **❸** is the best answer. For this to work, though, you'd better always act as if it's true and keep a distance between you and all Syrian men.

SITUATION 6

You're a Western woman walking down the street of a Syrian city and you pass a couple of young men you don't know. One of them says "Hello" to you and asks (in English) where you're from. You should:

❹ return the greeting, tell him where you came from, and stop to chat.
❸ look at him but don't respond.
❻ say "Hello" and continue walking.
❹ pretend you heard nothing.

The Best Choice

This is a difficult one because you're in another country and, as a guest, don't want to be rude. But you must protect yourself and your reputation (the latter may sound a bit old-fashioned, but is true there). The best choice is **❹**, even though this may seem unnecessarily rude; this is exactly what a Syrian woman would do. Choice **❸** is all right, but why even look at him? It will probably only encourage him, and **❻** would do so even more. Choosing **❹**, of course, would be the worst possible thing to do. It would only confirm a negative perception of Western women and might get you a lot of harassment and attempts to get physical with you. Give them an inch…

SITUATION 7

You're a woman walking in a souk, and you feel a hand brush across your buttocks, or worse yet, grab a buttock, breast or your crotch. You should:

A turn around, figure out who did it, scream as loudly as you can and attack the greaseball with your purse, fists, feet or anything else within easy reach.

B ignore it and move away quickly.

C find the man who did it and ask him why.

D find a police officer and tell him.

The Best Choice

The first choice is the only good one. Even though many men here do such things (particularly to Western women) others are embarrassed by the behaviour and the culprit himself is likely to feel humiliated if you attack him. If you are in a crowded place, there's almost no chance he'll fight back, and someone else is likely to come to your assistance. The worst choice is **B**; it will only encourage him to do it more often. **C** would be patently stupid and **D** is unlikely to accomplish anything at all. Even if the cop understands, he's not likely to do anything about it; even if he is willing to try, the molester will have vanished by then.

SITUATION 8

You drop off your suit at a dry-cleaner's and ask to have it the next night. You return the next evening when the proprietor said he'd be open, but the shop is closed. You wait for half an hour, and finally the adolescent son of the owner opens the shop. You're still learning Arabic, don't speak it well, and he doesn't understand a word of your native language. You have a date with a group to go to a concert in less than an hour. You should:

A chew him out in your best Arabic, ask him where the hell his father is, and demand your suit immediately.

B ask him if any of his neighbours speak English, get a translator, and let him know assertively but politely that

you must have the suit, and tell him you'll wait for it.
- **C** tell him you will come back in half an hour to get it.
- **D** find out when his father will be in and sit down and wait.

The Best Choice

A is the worst choice because time is not urgent in Syria, 'telling someone off' who didn't keep a promise is of little value, and you can't do it effectively anyway in a language you barely know. You're more likely to say something completely wrong and either insult the young man or utterly confuse him. Remember that he 'only works there' and that his father runs the shop. Choices **C** is likely to work only if you're lucky. If you come back in half an hour, the suit might still not be there; all sorts of shops send part of their work out to others when they're too busy for the job. As for **D**, the father might either arrive much later than his son expects or not at all. The only choice that is likely to work is **B**. At any rate, if you sit down to wait, the young man will do your work first or call the shop that has your suit to expedite it. He'll probably serve you tea while you wait, and instead of making an enemy you will have maintained a relationship that will probably be better in the future. Personal relationships count for more than anything else in Syrian culture.

SITUATION 9

You receive a notice that you have a package waiting for you at the post office and you arrive half an hour before closing time. You can't speak Arabic very well and you can't read it at all, so you stand in the shortest line you see. When you get to the window and show the clerk your notice, he speaks rapidly and motions for you to go to another window. You go to this window and wait in line for a long time. After your turn comes, the clerk walks off for a few minutes, comes back and starts to close his window, points at the clock which now says it's five minutes after closing time, and tells you to come back tomorrow. You should:

Ⓐ say "Please," and offer him 50 or 100 lira.

Ⓑ cause a scene and demand your package, telling him you've been waiting for 35 minutes already.

Ⓒ demand to see his boss.

Ⓓ just walk away, cursing to yourself.

The Best Choice

What many expats (and some Syrians) would do in this situation is **Ⓐ**. Hourly workers there earn less than enough to buy groceries for a family, and low-level government employees make less than most. You may run into a similar predicament when you're trying to get an exit visa or complete some other bureaucratic procedure. Instead of viewing the socio-economic phenomena of 'tipping' people to do their jobs with moral indignation, you'll be better off, get more accomplished in less time, and experience less frustration overall if you accept it as part of a culture that's very different from your own. Choice **Ⓑ** will get you nowhere, make you look foolish, and make an enemy of someone you may have to deal with regularly in the future. **Ⓒ** might work, depending on whether or not his boss is on the job and what kind of a person he is, but you may get the same answer from him: "We're closed now, come back tomorrow." And **Ⓓ** will only raise your blood pressure for you still have to come back tomorrow!

SITUATION 10

Someone you don't know well has invited you over for dinner. You're so impressed with the hospitality that you think you should take some kind of gift. An appropriate gift would be:

Ⓐ a bottle of expensive French wine you picked up on your last trip out of Syria.

Ⓑ nothing.

Ⓒ some of the chocolate chip cookies you just made so you can show them a favourite North American treat.

Ⓓ a bouquet of flowers.

The Best Choice

Choice **B** is acceptable, but **D** is an appreciated gesture. **A** and **C** would be the worst thing to do because 1) if they're Muslim, a gift of alcohol will be anything but appreciated and 2) any gift of food or drink taken to someone's home implies that you think your hosts' food and drink will not be good enough. The cookies are a good idea when you have Syrians to your home for a meal or treat, however.

SITUATION 11

A Syrian you know has invited you to his or her home twice and you've been unable to accept because of previous engagements, being out of town, or some other valid reason. The person invites you for a third time and you've just bought tickets for a concert that night. The best thing to do is:

A tell the person about the concert and ask if he or she and family would like to go along with you.

B accept the invitation and give the tickets to someone else.

C say you're sorry again but just can't make it.

D ask if you could come over the following evening.

The Best Choice

To some extent, this depends on how you feel about your would-be host. If it is someone you like and you feel badly about bowing out on the first two invitations, **B** is your answer (concert tickets are cheap anyway). If it's someone you're not fond of and don't want to get any closer to, **C** is the correct action; it may puzzle the Syrian, but you probably won't receive any more invitations. Neither **A** nor **D** are viable choices unless it's someone you know extremely well and who is not terribly traditional. Invitations aren't something you negotiate.

SITUATION 12

You've come to know a Syrian fairly well, and he asks you confidentially what you think of the country's leadership. The best response is:

A to be honest if you don't like the government.

B tell him you think they've done a good job of bringing Syria into the modern world, even if you don't believe it.

C tell him you don't know enough about it to discuss it.

D tell him you hate politics and don't even think about it unless you have to.

The Best Choice

Choices **B**, **C** and **D** are all realistic, and there's some truth to **B**. **A** should be avoided unless your honest feelings about the government are positive. The danger here is not so much that you will get into trouble as that your comments will be heard by the wrong person and your friend might get into trouble.

SITUATION 13

You receive an invitation to the wedding of a Syrian friend. You want to go, of course, but it's during your vacation and you plan on being out of the country. What should you do?

Ⓐ Apologise profusely but explain that you're going to be out of town at that time.

Ⓑ Rearrange your plans to accommodate the wedding.

Ⓒ Tell him/her you really want to come and ask if the date could be changed.

The Best Choice

Unless you've already bought non-refundable plane tickets, there's only one acceptable response in that culture—**Ⓑ**. If you've already bought tickets, then **Ⓐ** is acceptable. **Ⓒ** is a joke, of course, given the amount of time, planning and the involvement of both families that go into a wedding. Remember, there is no event as revered and as eagerly anticipated as a wedding, so to miss that of a good friend would be interpreted as lack of caring and respect. You would also miss a unique cultural experience that is worth a sacrifice.

SITUATION 14

A Syrian you've made friends with drops by unexpectedly at a time when you're really not in the mood to entertain and it is clear that he or she expects to be invited in. What should you do?

Ⓐ Exchange pleasantries at the door, excuse yourself, and ask your friend to drop back at another specific time.

Ⓑ Invite your friend in for tea, have a chat, then ask her to come back again sometime.

Ⓒ Invite your friend in for tea, have a chat, then ask him to call you before dropping by the next time.

Ⓓ Tell the person it would be better to phone before coming by.

The Best Choice

This happens a lot when Syrians know where you live (they do this to each other regularly). Even though most are aware that such visits are not common in your culture, they may think you won't mind if you've become friends. Although **❶** would be good cultural information for Syrians, it's simply too rude and would make your friends think you disliked them. The other three choices would all be acceptable, depending on your circumstances at the time. Excusing yourself at the moment but asking visitors to return later (at a specific time) will take the edge off your apparent lack of warmth in not inviting them in. You may get more than you bargain for if you pick **❷** since the visitor might take you at your word and really drop by any time and all the time, unannounced. I think **❸** is the best action, because it extends hospitality yet gives your friend a gentle hint that you prefer not to have people drop in unexpectedly.

SITUATION 15

You try to cross a street, and cars come at you from all directions, refusing to allow you to get across. What really bothers you, though, is that they all honk their horns at you. You find this so rude, you:

❶ give them the middle-finger salute.

❷ run across the street at the first slight break in traffic.

❸ step in front of an oncoming car, holding your hand up in a 'stop' command.

❹ wait until the street is clear.

The Best Choice

If you consistently follow **❹**, although it may be the safest action, you will spend most of your waking hours waiting to cross streets. The gesture in **❶** 'giving someone the finger' is not used here (but it is understood, thanks to American movies and TV programmes) and may get you into a fight. **❷** is all right, but you might throw off the 'aim' of a driver: people here don't run across streets, and most drivers are amazingly accurate at driving toward you as you walk across the street, passing only inches behind you. This leaves **C** as the best choice, because your signal to the driver will almost always be honoured. Remember, the one in front (pedestrian or vehicle) has the right of way, if only for a moment.

SITUATION 16

You are driving on the four-lane, divided highway between Damascus and Homs, in the inside lane, passing several slower-moving vehicles. You are going quite fast, but another car comes flying up behind you, riding on your rear bumper and flashing its lights. You noticed it when it was still a quarter of a kilometre back, and its lights were flashing then, too. You decide to:

A teach the jerk a lesson for his rudeness and refuse to pull over, staying beside one of the vehicles you're passing.

B the same as above, but also give him the finger.

C pull over, even though you haven't finished passing the vehicles, and let him by.

D ignore him and continue in the passing lane until you're past the string of vehicles, then pull over.

The Best Choice

The only thing worse than **A** would be **B**! I know of people who tried **A** and ended up getting beaten for refusing to let someone pass. One of the unwritten rules of the road here is that you let drivers pass when they beep their horns or flash their lights, or both. The best action is **C**, although you can probably get away with **D** as long as you don't take too long.

SITUATION 17

You're walking into a government building, embassy or foreign cultural centre, and the soldier guarding the entrance stops you, says something in Arabic you don't understand, holds out a hand with the palm up and draws the outside edge of his other hand in a cutting motion across his wrist. He is indicating that:

Ⓐ he wants *baksheesh* to let you in.

Ⓑ your hand will be cut off if you steal anything.

Ⓒ he wants to see your passport.

Ⓓ he wants your ticket to enter.

The Answer

Although **Ⓐ** is a common expectation here, *baksheesh* isn't asked for in such an obvious way. **Ⓑ** isn't correct: Syria doesn't apply Islamic law that requires this punishment. Even if you needed a ticket to enter a building or compound, the soldier wouldn't be the one collecting tickets, so **Ⓓ** is wrong. This gesture is used to ask for your passport. You can also use it in a restaurant when you see your waiter across the room and want your bill. A similar gesture, but with the edge of a hand drawn across the inside of the elbow, means a large piece of paper or a notebook.

DO'S AND DON'TS

DO'S

- Dress modestly. Neither sex should wear shorts or sleeveless shirts. Women should wear a long skirt or loose pants and long-sleeved shirts. You should also bring a long scarf to cover your head in mosques. Although you do not need to go veiled all the time, some women will feel more comfortable if they wear a veil in certain situations or neighbourhoods. Men should also dress modestly. Jeans are okay, but keep in mind that most Syrian men dress up.
- Do your best to learn a few words in Arabic (See Chapter 8), especially if you'll be in the country for several months or longer. They will go a long way in making some friends and in making your stay more pleasant.
- Learn to read Arabic numbers. It is fairly easy and will make your time in Syria much easier and more pleasant, especially where money matters are concerned. Practice by reading license plate numbers (which also have Western equivalents) while you are riding the bus or service taxi.
- Carry small treats for children, such as pens, candy and key chains, when visiting Syria's more popular tourist attractions. Syrian children are generally sweet and well-behaved, and these small trinkets cross language barriers, and make the kids very happy.
- Remember that Islam forbids the consumption of alcohol. Public drunkenness is generally frowned upon, so if you do take a drink, do so in moderation. If you want to get smashed, do so in the privacy of your own home.
- Avoid eye contact with men you do not know personally if you are a woman. Arab men sometimes interpret (albeit wrongly) glances by Western women to be invitations for sex or hints that they desire the men.
- Ignore any lewd comments that local men might make if you are a woman. If a man touches you inappropriately, however, you should raise a commotion and draw attention

to him or call for the police. Chances are the people nearby will come to your rescue.

- Make sure to tip busboys and assistants in restaurants. They do not get a share of the waiter's tip, even though they do just as much work. A 10 per cent tip for waiters is fine, and a few Syrian coins will suffice for the busboys and assistants.
- Take extra care when crossing the street, especially in larger cities like Damascus and Aleppo. Pedestrians do not have Western-style right of way in Syria.

DON'TS

- Be loud or do anything to stand out in public—unless you're the victim of a crime or groping. Syrians prefer blending in to standing out. In fact, if you are harassed, making a scene usually causes the offender to back off out of embarrassment.
- Sit with the sole of your shoe facing someone. This is considered very bad behaviour throughout the Arab world, since the sole of the shoe is considered one of the dirtiest places. Always sit with both feet on the floor.
- Cross your legs or ankles or place your feet on tables or footstools. When seated on the ground or floor, sit in such a manner that your soles are hidden.
- Eat or shake hands with your left hand. It is considered unclean in Arab countries, since the left hand usually is reserved for toilet activities.
- Get into conversations about politics or national issues with strangers. They could be the Mukhabarat (secret police). To avoid trouble, it is best to give noncommittal answers to any questions from strangers and always with a positive spin.
- Refuse an invitation to a cup of tea if you can help it. If you do, you will certainly miss out on the opportunity to gain a first-hand look at Syrian life and culture. If you must refuse (which is usually considered impolite), put your hand over your heart while you decline to show that no harm is meant. You might need to repeat this gesture several times.

- Take anyone's photo without first asking for their permission. (This rule applies in every country, but it bears repeating.) This is especially true for photos of women.
- Throw toilet paper in the toilets of most old buildings. It will clog their plumbing systems, since Syrian pipes are generally too narrow to accommodate paper. Instead, toss the paper in the small wastebaskets placed near the toilets for this purpose.
- Sit next to a member of the opposite sex whom you do not know. On a bus, for example, if the only available seat is next to a woman, it would be more culturally acceptable to stand.
- Bring food or beverages as a gift when you are invited to eat at a Syrian's home. If you do so, they will think that you anticipate that their food will taste bad. Above all, never bring a bottle of wine or alcohol, since Muslims do not drink alcoholic beverages! It is acceptable not to bring anything. If you do wish to bring a gift, bring a small bouquet of flowers.
- Be insulted or put off if someone stares at you. It is quite acceptable behaviour for Syrians to stare. Even when you wear modest clothes and demonstrate the most impeccable manners, you will probably be stared at and attract attention.
- Engage in public displays of affection, like hand-holding, hugging or kissing, with your spouse or boyfriend/girlfriend. This is frowned upon in Syria. On the other hand, public displays of affection between members of the same sex are quite acceptable.

GLOSSARY

Al Assad, Lake	Syria's largest body of water, formed by Tabaqah Dam on Euphrates near Aleppo
Al Hamdulla	most common response to greeting of "How are you?" meaning praise Allah!
Al Jazeera	triangle of land northeast of Euphrates and al Khabur Rivers; meaning island
Alawites	Muslims originally from mountains of northwestern Syria with somewhat mysterious beliefs and rites
Alexandretta	northwestern corner of Syria given to Turkey by French; also called Hatay Peninsula
Arab coffee	boiled with coffee grounds and powdered cardamom at bottom of pot; served in demitasse with lots of sugar; dense and strong
Arabian Gulf	what Arabs call the Persian Gulf
Aramaeans	one of the first known groups of Semitic peoples to settle east of coastal mountains
Arram, Lake	one of only two natural lakes in Syria; fills crater of extinct volcano in Golan Heights
Arwad	Syria's only island; ancient Phoenician base
Assyrians	ancient peoples from eastern area; Syria named from them; were well known for military conquests and brutality

Baab	Arabic word for gate; part of many names for areas of old cities
Babylonians	ancient peoples from what is now a part of Iraq; Babylon is the ancient name of Baghdad
Baksheesh	tip or bribe; line of distinction obscured in Syrian culture
Ba'ath Party	socialistic Pan-Arab party in Syria and Iraq; founded by one Christian and one Muslim man; Syria's only viable political party
Bedouin	original nomadic Arabs
Bukra, insha'allah	"Tomorrow, maybe"; common response when answer to inquiry is unknown
CBS	Commerical Bank of Syria
Caliph	top leader of early Islam (Sunni), after death of Mohammed
Canaanites	ancient peoples who moved onto coastal plain and seaward side of mountains of Levant; essentially beginning of area's known history
Children of The Book	Muslim expression for themselves, Jews and Christians
Cola	used by Syrians to mean any type of soda pop
Correctionist Movement	Hafez al-Assad's name for his coup and following government; claimed that al-Asad's immediate predecessor erred in support for communist-type collective farms, economy run completely by national government and support for Palestinian struggle at expense of Syria's own well-being; movement to 'correct' these mistakes

Crusaders	French Catholics who travelled to Levant with intent of taking back Jerusalem for Christianity; slaughtered many men, women and children in their quest
Damashq	Arabic name for Damascus
Druze	offshoot Muslim group in southern Syria and northern Jordan
Eid al-Adha	festival following traditional end of *Hajj* (pilgrimage to Mecca)
Eid al-Fitr	festival immediately following the end of Ramadan
Euphrates	main river in Syria (in east); shared by Turkey, Syria and Iraq
Falaafel sandwich	Arab-style vegetable burrito
Fatteh	concoction vaguely similar to hot breakfast cereal
Fejera wa jwazaat	Arabic name for passport and immigration (P&I) office
Fertile Crescent	name for Mesopotamia; area between Tigris and Euphrates Rivers from mountains of the north to the Persian Gulf
Five Pillars of Islam	five beliefs/practices essential to practice of Islam
Fool	fava beans cooked in oil, lemon juice and garlic, topped with yogurt; eaten for breakfast
Free Zones	areas in Syria where investments are particularly liberalised and encouraged
Gharb Depression	valley between coastal and inland mountains

Hajj	one of Five Pillars, pilgrimage to Mecca with stop in Medina to pay respects at Prophet's grave; required at least once in lifetime if person has financial means; some make pilgrimage many times, others pay for poorer friends/relatives to make trip; official time is during days seven to ten of the 12th month of the Islamic year
Haleb	Arabic name for Aleppo
Hatay Peninsula	northwestern corner of Syria given by French to Turkey; also called Alexandretta
Hittites	ancient peoples who invaded Syria from north; from what is now area of Turkey
Hommus	dipping paste made from chick peas, *tahini* (sesame paste), lemon and garlic
Iftar	evening meal that breaks day's fast during Ramadan
Insha'allah	most common expression used when Arabs talk about future plans; meaning Allah willing
Investment Law No.10	put into effect in early 1991 and amended in 2000; begins to change Syria's centralised economic control
Iqaama	residency permit
Kabob	spiced, minced lamb pressed into weiner shape on a skewer
Kafeeyeh	men's headdress with either red and white or black and white pattern; made world-famous by Yasar Arafat

Karnak	Syria's intercity bus system
Kibbeh	meat pie made with ground lamb, bulgur and seasonings
Kurds	group of people without own homeland; living area covers parts of northern Syria, Iraq, Iran and southern Turkey
Leban	Arabic word for both yogurt and a drink made from yogurt
Levant, the	area that is now Syria, Lebanon, the Alexandretta (part of Turkey), Palestine, Israel and Jordan; also sometimes called Greater Syria
Lira	another word for Syrian pound
Mamluks	Egyptians who partially colonised the Levant after the Crusaders were driven out
Mesopotamia	area between the Tigris and Euphrates Rivers from mountains of the north to what is now Persian Gulf; also called the Fertile Crescent
Mt. Qassioun	small mountain against which Damascus snuggles on the east side
Mtabbal	eggplant, yogurt and garlic dip
Mukhabarat	the secret police
Mzerib, Lake	one of only two natural lakes in Syria; northeast of Der'a, near border with Jordan
Omayyads	initially strongest of Arab clans after death of Mohammed; started and ruled Arab empire from Syria; less dogmatic than other Muslim groups and more socially and politically oriented

Ottoman empire	empire of the Turkish Ottomans, extending from Arab Peninsula to Europe and North Africa
Pal	type of video system used in Syria; Pal and NTSC (North American) tapes will not play on machines intended for the other
Palmyra	ruins of ancient Rome in the central desert of Syria
People's Assembly	nominal legislative body of Syrian government
Phoenicians	first great seafarers of Mediterranean, so named by the Greeks, although they didn't call themselves that; name simply referred to all peoples of the area
Piastres	100 piastres per Syrian pound
Ramadan	annual month-long fast required by Islam
SAR	Syrian Arab Republic; Syria's official name
SP	Syrian pounds; also sometimes called lira
Salah al-Din	Arab famous for driving French Crusaders out of Levant with assistance of Mamluks from Egypt
Salat	One of Five Pillars: prayer five times daily—at sunrise, midday, afternoon, sunset and evening. Prayers prescribed in both form and content

Sawm	One of Five Pillars: fasting during Ramadan, ninth month of the Islamic year; no food, drinks (even water), smoking, or sex from before dawn til after sunset; begins and ends—according to the instructions of the Koran—when one cannot distinguish white thread from black thread in natural light; also allows those travelling during Ramadan to fast at other time; purposes of fast are to purify soul and body and focus one's attention on God; in Syrian cities, beginning and end of fast are marked by cannons firing.
Service taxis	intercity taxis
Shaawarma	Arab chicken or lamb burrito-type food
Shahada	One of Five Pillars: declaration that there is only one God and that Mohammed was his last prophet
Sheikh	leader of a mosque, so chosen because of his Koranic scholarship and perceived piety
Shi'ites, Shi'a	Muslim minority that argued that after death of Mohammed the new leader had to be a family member of the prophet; chose Ali, his nephew; in perpetual conflict with Sunni
Soda	Syrian word for liver
Souk	traditional Arab market place; very lively with lots of scents and sounds

Sumerians (of what is now southern Iraq)	ancient peoples who eventually moved into what is now Syria
Sunnis	Muslim majority who wanted to appoint Caliphs to rule in Mohammed's place after his death; in perpetual conflict with the Shi'a
Syrian Desert	covers most of Jordan, Iraq and northern Saudi Arabia as well
Tabouleh	traditional Middle-Eastern salad made with parsley, bulgar wheat, cucumbers, tomatoes, green onions, lemon juice and olive oil
Ugarit	area of ruins in northwestern Syria where one of first-known alphabets was discovered
United Arab Republic (UAR)	union of Syria and Egypt from 1958 until 1961
Yalanji	grape leaves stuffed with spiced mixture of ground lamb and rice
Zakat	one of Five Pillars: annual tithe of 2.5 per cent of earnings above basic necessities; money used to build and maintain mosques and help the poor
Zionist Jews	European Jews whose explicit goal was to take back the Holy Land from Arabs; believed God gave them that land

RESOURCE GUIDE

EMERGENCIES AND HEALTH
Emergency Numbers
- **Ambulance** 110
- **Fire** 113
- **Police** 112

Damascus
- **Electric power repairs.** Tel: 222-3887
- **International operator.** Tel: 143/144
- **Local operator.** Tel: 147
- **Red Crescent** (Middle Eastern Red Cross). Tel: 333-1441 or 333-0755.

Hospitals/Medical Services
Damascus
- **Shami Hospital**. Tel: 373-5090/1/2/3/4/5 or 373-4925/6/7
- **Italian Hospital** Tel 332-9404 or 332-6030/1

Aleppo
- **Ummal al-Najilt Pharmacy** Near entrance of Baghdad Station. Open 24 hours. Tel: 225-1478.

HOME AND FAMILY
Schools
- **Damascus Community School**
  Tel: 333-7737 or 333-0331/2

Budget Hotels
Damascus
- **Hotel Al-Majed** 29 Ayar Street, behind Cinema Alsofara. Tel: 232-3300.
- **Sultan Hotel** Moussallam Baroudi Rd, west of Hejaz Railroad Station. Tel: 222-5768.
- **Grand Ghazi Hotel** Furat Avenue. Tel: 221-4581.

Aleppo
- **Ramsis Hotel** Baron Street. Tel: 211-1102.
- **Hotel Al-Raoudah** Al-Maari Street. Tel: 233-896.

- **Beit Wakil** Sissi Street. Tel: 221-7169, 211-8169 or 211-7083

MANAGING YOUR MONEY
Insurance
If you want health insurance, you should either procure it in your country of origin before travelling to Syria or buy an international policy through a Western insurance company after you arrive.

Cash
The Syrian pound is the official currency. Traveller's cheques are generally only accepted at 3-star hotels, travel agencies, rental car agencies and a few larger shops. It is also useful to bring US$ 1 and US$ 10 bills, especially for shopping in the souks. More companies accept credit cards now, but some charge an extra fee to process a transaction using one.

Banking
Damascus
- **Commercial Bank of Syria** Martyr's Square/Hejaz Railway Station/Youssef al-Azmeh Square.

Aleppo
- **Commercial Bank of Syria** Baron Street. Open daily except on Fridays, from 8:30–1:30 pm.

Exchanging Money
Damascus
- **American Express** Small alley off Fardous Street, in a Sudan Airways office. Tel: 224-6500, 222-3708 or 222-1756
- **Nahas Travel (Thomas Cook)** Fardous Street.

Aleppo
Exchange booths are located at Kouwatli and Bab al-Faraj Streets. Open daily except Fridays, from 8 am–7:30 pm.

Borrowing Money
You can borrow money from the Commercial Bank of Syria. Check at branches for current rates. If you need to borrow a small amount of money, it is much easier to get a cash advance from a credit card. Also, there are numerous new

private banks, but each has its own lending policies, so check with several and compare.

ENTERTAINMENT AND LEISURE
Restaurants
Damascus
- **Abu al'Izz Restaurant** In Souk al Hamediyah; dripping with atmosphere and often has live music. Tel: 221-8174.
- **Bourj al-Roos** Rustic, serves great fish; inexpensive, too.
- **Haretna** Baab Touma area. Great *mezzeh* and *kebobs*. Trendy and fashionable as well. Tel: 544-1148. www.haretna.net
- **Il Circo** In Four Seasons Hotel. Tel: 339-1000. Italian food in comfy surroundings, great service and great wine selection; serves good seafood.
- **Nadi al Sharq** Next to Amideast. Indian cuisine, maybe best in Damascus.
- **Nadil** Near Bab Sharqi. Spicy. On Abu Roumaneh side of Jisr al-Abiad—homemade Arab food
- **Narcissus Palace** Old City. Located in an old Damascene house built in 1735. Great shish kebabs. Tel: 543-1205 or 541-6785.
- **Old Damascus Restaurant** Behind the Citadel. Tel: 221-8810.
- **Orient Club** Across from Four Seasons Hotel. Tel: 245-9225. Great traditional cuisine.
- **Reef Restaurant** Abu Roumaneh Street. Tel: 333-2830 or 333-1973.
- **Sharia Medhat Pasha** At the turn to Baab Kisan. Good pizza and pasta, although some don't like the service.
- **Scoozi** Maysaloun Street, Abu Roumaneh. Tel: 333-2410 or 331-0511. Bright European café with fantastic service. www.scoozi-sy.com
- **Umayyad Palace** Around corner from Umayyad Mosque. Tel: 222-0826.

Aleppo
- **Al Andalib** Baron Street. Tel: 222-4030.
- **Beit Wakil** Sissi Street. Tel: 221-7169 or 224-7083. Wonderful decor, great food and service. They also have a beautiful hotel.

Cafés
Damascus

- **An-Nawafara** Turn right at Umayyad Mosque wall, take the first right and the café will be on your right. Tel: 543-6813. Single women should feel at ease here.
- **Café la Terasse** Between Baab Sharqi and Ananias mansion.
- **Inhouse Coffee** A chain at the airport and other locations. Great European-style coffee. Tel: 333-6039.
- **Vienna Café** Near Cham Palace, turn opposite Adidas store. Dark bread sandwiches and apple strudel, among other things.

Aleppo

- **Patisserie Mousattat** Next to exchange booth on Baab al-Faraj Street. Tel: 212-747. Gooey Middle Eastern pastries.

Shopping Districts
Damascus

- **Old City. Souq al-Hamidiyah** Near Umayyad Mosque, this souk sprawls for blocks. Make note of where you enter.

Aleppo

- **Souq ash-Shouna** Located near base of the Citadel. Seven miles of souks! Different items are located on different blocks, i.e. gold, rugs, spices, etc.

Nightspots
Damascus

- **Backdoor** At Barada Sports Club in Mazrah. Trendy dance hall for R&B and Arab pop. Entrance fee of 1,000 SP.
- **Domino** Bar and café in Baab Touma. Becomes disco after 11pm.
- **Piano Bar** Near Café la Terasse, between Baab Sharqi and Ananias mansion. Tel: 543-0375.
- **Mar Mar** Near Bakri baths in Baab Touma. Owner performs with own funk band regularly.

Bookshops
Damascus

- **Librairie Avicenne** One block south of the Cham Palace Hotel. Tel: 221-2911.

- **Librairie Universelle** Port Said and Basha Streets. Tel: 230-0744.

Aleppo

- **Librairie Said** Qostaki Homsi and Litani Streets.

Music

Music is a part of café life in Damascus. You also can attend all kinds of performances at Damascus' **Al Hamra Street Theatre**. Check in the English language *Syria Times* for current listings.

Dance

Dance—except for men spontaneously dancing alone or with each other—is not a huge component of Syrian life. You can see traditional Syrian dances, whirling dervishes and acrobatic sword dances at the **Umayyad Restaurant** in Damascus. Although it is a bit touristy, it gives you a fun flavour of the culture and Syrian spirit and enthusiasm—all while you stuff yourself with scrumptious Syrian cuisine.

Alternative Lifestyles

Homosexuality is illegal in Syria and even imposes a prison sentence. If you are gay, keeping a low profile is a good idea if you want to avoid trouble while in Syria.

TRANSPORT AND COMMUNICATIONS
Country and City Telephone Codes

- **Country code:** 963
- **City codes:**

Aleppo	21	Damascus	11
Hama	33	Homs	31
Lattakia	41	Palmyra	34

Telephone Service

The telephone office is located one block east of Hejaz Railway on An-Nasr Avenue. It is open 24 hours. You can buy Easycomm phonecards at the post office.

Internet Facilities and Cafés
Damascus
- **Public Internet Hall** Muhajrine neighbourhood
- **Assad National Library** (run by the Ministry of Culture)
- **Zoni Internet Service** Tel: 232-4670
- **Sky Net** Badawi and Janan Bldg near Al Hamra Road. Tel: 331-2372.

Post Offices
Damascus
- Said al-Jabri Ave
  Open daily from 8 am–7 pm. Tel: 221-9000.

Aleppo
- Square across Kouwatli Street
  Open daily from 8 am–5 pm. Also offers a fax service.

Newspapers and Magazines
A variety of Arabic newspapers are available. A Communist newspaper, *Sawt al-Shaab* (People's Voice), Syria's first non-governmentally controlled paper, was introduced in January 2001. For English-language papers, there is *Syria Times. The Middle East, International Herald Tribune, Le Monde, Der Spiegel* and *Newsweek* can also be found in most larger towns and cites.

Television
- **Syrian Broadcast Service**
  English news runs on Syria 2 at 10 pm.
- **British Broadcasting Corporation (BBC)**
- Turkish TV can be seen in some northern towns. Jordanian TV is available in the south. Satellite TV recommended.

LANGUAGE
The official language is Arabic but some people speak French or English.
Language Institutes and Classes
- **Arabic Language Center (ALC)** of The Language Institute at Damascus University. Mezzeh Highway Fayez Mansour St.

—Campus of Humanities. Tel: 392-5843. Fax: 212-0164. E-mail: inquiries@arabicindamascus.edu.sy
- **Arabic Teaching Institute for Foreigners** Jadet ash-Shafei 3, Meezeh-Villat Sharqiyyah. Tel: 222-1538.

GENERAL COUNTRY INFORMATION
Appliances and Utilities
The electrical system is nominally 220 volts (but often less in reality) and 50 cycles. North America uses 60 cycles. This difference makes most North American appliances run more slowly here, so if you bring any electrical items with you from North America, make sure they can run with both 50 and 60 cycles.

Necessities and Documents to Bring
All foreign citizens need a visa, available in Syrian consulates outside of the country. You can also sometimes get them at border crossings and airports. Visas are valid for up to 15 days. Always bring photocopies of your passport, credit cards and other important documents in case they are lost or stolen. If you have any evidence of an Israeli stamp in your passport, you will not be allowed in Syria.

Consider bringing:
- Small packets of tissue paper (toilet paper is not always available in public restrooms)
- Contraceptives other than condoms (difficult to buy in Syria)
- An extra flat sheet (Some hotels do not provide top sheets)
- Any medicines you might need. Make sure they are in the original prescription bottles.

For Women
Women should bring tampons, since they are hard to come by and expensive. Also, bring a veil so you can visit mosques, long-sleeved shirts and long skirts. If you are single or travelling alone, wearing a wedding band (real or faux) is a good idea.

Pre-Entry Vaccinations

Though none are required, consult with your doctor before leaving. He may recommend booster shots. Getting inoculations for hepatitis A and B and typhoid, however, is probably a prudent idea. If you are entering Syria from sub-Saharan Africa or any other area that has been infected, you may need to get a vaccination for yellow fever.

EMBASSIES IN SYRIA

- **Australia** Consular services for Australian citizens provided by Canadian embassy in Damascus.
- **Canada** Lot 12, Autostrade Mezzeh. Tel: 611-6692 (24 hrs). Email: dmcus@international.gc.ca
- **France** Ata Al-Ayyoubi Street. Tel: 339-0200.
- **Germany** Abdulmunen Al-Riad Street, corner Ebla Street. Tel: 379-0000.
- **Great Britain** Mohammed Kurd Ali Street, Kotob Building. Tel: 339-1513 or 339-1541 (consular)
- **Italy** 82 Al-Ayyoubi Street. Tel: 333-8338.
- **Japan** 3537 Sharkasiya, Aljala' Street, Abu Romaneh. Tel: 333-8273 or 333-2553.
- **USA** 2 Al-Mansour Street, Abu Romaneh. Tel: 3391-4444 (After hours: 3391-3333)

Government Internet Web Sites

- http://www.visit-syria.com.
- http://www.syriatourism.org.

General/Tourist Advice Bureaus and Websites

- **http://cafe-Syria.com**
  The ultimate web resource for those who want to learn more about Syria. It features the latest news, cultural, travel, historical and technological information on Syria.

Damascus

- **Tourist Office**
  29 Mai Avenue. Open daily from 9 am–7 pm.
- **Ministry of Tourism**
  Near Takiyyeh as-Salaymaniyyeh Mosque.
  Open from Saturday–Thursday, from 9 am–2 pm.

BUSINESS INFORMATION
Business Organisations

- **Federation of Syrian Chambers of Commerce.**
  Mousa Bin Nusair Street, opposite Meridian Hotel,
  PO Box 5909, Damascus. Tel: 333-7344 or 331-1504.
  Fax: 333-1127. www.fedcommsyr.org.
  Email: syr-trade@mail.sy
- **Aleppo Chamber of Commerce.**
  Extension of the Central Bank, PO Box 1261, Aleppo.
  Tel: 223-8237 or 223-8236. Fax: 221-3493.

Career Services

- **Future Corp**
  Kouwalti Street, PO Box 2402, Latakia, Syria.
  Tel: 240-7777. Fax: 230-7777.
  Email: info@futurehrs.com

Legal Matters

It is best to avoid trouble, since Syrian legal matters are not always handled expeditiously, clearly, and in accord with international standards. The country houses many political prisoners who have no say over their fates. Amnesty International has condemned the country for its numerous human rights violations. If you find yourself in trouble, you should try to hire a private attorney and consult your country's embassy.

FURTHER READING

Good books on Syria (translated into English) are difficult to come by, unless you live near a university that has a good Middle Eastern studies programme. Most libraries seem to have only a few titles specifically about Syria, most of them quite outdated or written by ex-CIA operatives in Syria or other United States government programmes. Needless to say, the latter are not the most reliable sources of information in view of the decades-long animosity of the US government toward Syria, the general ignorance of Americans about life in the Middle East (particularly in Syria), and the general American attitude that Israel wears the white hat and Syria wears a black one.

The following books give the best, most complete picture of Syrian history, culture and life that I have been able to find. Websites, however, are perhaps the best source of up-to-date info about the country, so I have included quite a number of those that I found both useful and interesting.

BOOKS

The Hidden Face of Eve: Women in the Arab World. Al Saadawi, Nawal. Translated by Sherif Hetata, foreword by Irene L Gendizier. Boston: Beacon Press, 1982.
- Ms Al Saadawi was raised in an upper-class Egyptian family, became a feminist and successful medical doctor, and eventually headed the Egyptian Ministry of Health. In this book she gives a brief history of the brutality practised on women in the Middle East both before and after Islam, including an account of her own clitoridectomy (commonly referred to by the euphemism 'female circumcision'). She also does not spare the views of women preached and practised by Christianity and the West in general. She has written several books, most of them not translated into English, and her 'radical' view that women are as capable as men and should be in all positions of leadership and her continuous criticism

of male hegemony in all areas of life have cost her her government position and a prison term.

Her views are Marxist, and she recommends collectivisation and other centralised controls that have since disintegrated in the former communist and heavily socialised countries. Despite this, most of her observations are poignant, and she writes predominantly from experience and first-hand knowledge, not a sterile academic perspective.

Monuments of Syria: A Historical Guide. Burns, Ross. London: I.B. Tauris & Co. Ltd., 1992.
- If you're an amateur archaeologist or simply want to enjoy many of the historical wonders of Syria, this book is a must. Road maps of the country are not very accurate: they do not show all the roads and villages, and the symbols they use for sites of historical and archaeological interest are only approximate. Because of this and the fact that road signs are scarce or illegible on all but major roads, it's not uncommon to spend an entire day looking for something you thought you could find in an hour or two. *Monuments* not only shows accurate routes to out-of-the-way ruins and dead cities, but it gives historical detail about each. Most of Syria's ruins are never seen by anyone except the native villagers or Bedouins who live near them. Some remains are even incorporated into village houses or are used as living quarters for villagers or nomads.

Trends and Issues in Contemporary Arab Thought. Boullata, Issa J. New York: SUNY Press, 1990.
- This book looks at broad, modern issues in Arab life, giving detailed descriptions of the views of many modern Arab scholars, selected by the author to represent the widest possible spectrum of contemporary Arab thought. Boullata gives as much time and space to the views of those who claim the only hope for the salvation and advancement of Arab culture is a return to the 'good old days' of early Islam as to those who wish to separate religion from government. One point all the scholars cited

agree on is that Arabs should not simply try to imitate the West; they all appreciate the uniqueness of their culture and wish to make scientific and economic progress in a manner consistent with their traditions.

The author also discusses the problems of intellectual freedom in autocratic Arab states and the often vast intellectual gulf between the Arab masses (most of whom live in poverty or near-poverty and are illiterate or barely literate) and the relative handful of Arab scholars.

The Venture of Islam: Conscience and History in a World Civilisation, Parts I, II, & III. Marshall, G S Hodgson. Chicago: University of Chicago Press, 1974.
- This is an encyclopedic study of the history of Islam. Although Syria *per se* is not discussed extensively, there are many references to it. The important point is that a prerequisite to understanding *any* Arab country requires knowledge of Islam and its development, teachings and influence on its culture. The writing style is academic, and I doubt that most people would want to sit down and read it like a novel; but it is a good reference source and selective readings of the work will increase your understanding of Arab culture in general.

Syria and Lebanon. Ziadeh, Nicola A. Lebanon: Librairie du Liban, 1968.
- Although this book is quite old, it gives an Arab's perspective on the historical development and domination of the Levant (with focus on Syrian and Lebanon), and therefore provides a valuable insight into Syrians' views of their part in Western history. Unlike most accounts of history read in the West, it is a perspective of those who have been dominated rather than the view of the colonisers.

WEBSITES
News
- http://www.syriadaily.com/
- http://www.cafe-syria.com

- http://news.bbc.co.uk/2/hi/middle_east/country_profiles/801669.stm
- http://www1.albawaba.com/en/country/Syria
- http://www.topix.net/world/syria
- http://www.syria-today.com

Government
- http://ec.europa.eu/external_relations/syria/index_en.htm
- http://www.gksoft.com/govt/en/sy.html
- http://www.hrw.org
- http://amarji.blogspot.com/2007/03/dying-of-old-damascus.html
- http://www.cbssyr.org/

Economy
- http://www.dci-syria.org/
- http://www.syria-report.com/
- http://www.doingbusiness.org/ExploreEconomies/?economyid = 183

History, Culture, Food, etc.
- http://lexicorient.com/e.o/syria.htm
- http://www.damascus-online.com/damascus
- http://www.oldamascus.com/home.htm
- http://www.worldstatesmen.org/Syria.html
- http://www.ameinfo.com/syria/
- http://almashriq.hiof.no/base/syria.html
- http://lcweb2.loc.gov/frd/cs/sytoc.html
- http://www.syriagate.com/
- http://www.talesmag.com/rprweb/the_rprs/mid_east/syria.shtml
- http://www.ethnologue.com/show_country.asp?name = Syria
- http://www.nytimes.com/2006/08/29/world/middleeast/29syria.html
- http://almashriq.hiof.no/syria/900/910/919/damas/old-city/abu-el-izz.html
- http://www.musicalmissions.com/syria.html
- http://www.theworldly.org/ArticlesPages/Articles2006/July06Articles/DamascusFoods.html

- http://www.travelpod.com/travel–photo/technotrekker/ overland05/1143018240/26-lunch.jpg/tpod.html
- http://www.travelpod.com/travel–photo/technotrekker/ overland05/1143018240/25-bus.jpg/tpod.html
- http://www.arabeskstudiesindamascus.com

Travel
- http://www.lonelyplanet/com/syria
- http://www.visit-syria.com/
- http://www.syriatourism.org/
- http://www.jordanjubilee.com/travelme/tosyria.htm

General
- http://www.ou.edu/ssa/general_info.htm
- http://www.syriaonline.com
- http://www.cia.gov/library/publications/the-world-factbook/geos/sy.html
- http://www.al-bab.com/arab/countries/syria.htm

ABOUT THE AUTHOR

Coleman South was raised in the western part of the United States and lived there until his early 40s, when he moved to Damascus, Syria. He earned a bachelor's degree in psychology in 1973, then worked in various occupations and professions over the next 17 years. He has always had a great desire to travel and live abroad, so in 1990 he left the bank where he was a vice-president and began work on a master's degree to teach English as a second language.

He has taught English in the United States and Syria, and has lived in Japan for more than 12 years and is Associate Professor of EFL at a university in southern Japan. He has also travelled in nearly 20 European, Middle Eastern and other Asian countries, and most of North America.

Coleman has written and published an illustrated book on Syria (*Cultures of the World: Syria*), another of the same on Jordan (*Cultures of the World: Jordan*—recently revised), another on US-Japanese comparative culture for Japanese students, a cultural guide for international students studying at the university where he taught in the United States, numerous travel and professional (English teaching) articles, poetry and short stories

INDEX

Titles in the CultureShock! series:

Argentina	France	Portugal
Australia	Germany	Russia
Austria	Great Britain	San Francisco
Bahrain	Hawaii	Saudi Arabia
Beijing	Hong Kong	Scotland
Belgium	India	Shanghai
Berlin	Ireland	Singapore
Bolivia	Italy	South Africa
Borneo	Jakarta	Spain
Brazil	Japan	Sri Lanka
Bulgaria	Korea	Sweden
Cambodia	Laos	Switzerland
Canada	London	Syria
Chicago	Malaysia	Taiwan
Chile	Mauritius	Thailand
China	Morocco	Tokyo
Costa Rica	Munich	Travel Safe
Cuba	Myanmar	Turkey
Czech Republic	Netherlands	United Arab
Denmark	New Zealand	Emirates
Ecuador	Pakistan	USA
Egypt	Paris	Vancouver
Finland	Philippines	Venezuela

For more information about any of these titles, please contact any of our Marshall Cavendish offices around the world (listed on page ii) or visit our website at:

www.marshallcavendish.com/genref